ARRIVE. DRIVE. THRIVE.

For Aspiring, Emerging, and Growing Leaders

EMPOWER YOUR LEADERSHIP

GERALD HUTCHINSON Ph.D.

NETTIE NITZBERG M.Ed.

JOSHUA SATERMAN

Printed in the United States of America
Published by Saterman Connect, LLC
ISBN number: 978-1-68524-229-9

Praise for Arrive. Drive. Thrive.™

Arrive. Drive. Thrive.™ is for the leader who is ready to do the work and wants to lead with equity and open-mindedness. ***Arrive. Drive. Thrive.™*** thoughtfully provides methods, concepts, and tools to lead with integrity, mindfulness, and awareness.

Mita Mallick, Head of Inclusion, Equity, and Impact, Carta

Your coach may get nervous (and excited) when they see a copy of ***Arrive. Drive. Thrive.™*** on your desk. Unlike most leadership texts, this book speaks to you through stories. ***Arrive. Drive. Thrive.™*** coaches you through your leadership journey using new and fresh frameworks accompanied by practical tips. This is an essential guide for all leaders whether new or 'tenured'. I will refer to this book several times a week because with ***Arrive. Drive. Thrive.™*** your leadership toolkit is accessible to utilise in everyday life. Your chances of being an effective leader just increased because of this book!

Lisa Moore, Head of Talent, Business Partnering and People Operations, Yahoo!

Arrive. Drive. Thrive.™ is a complete workbook and reference guide not just another leadership book. A go to resource for emerging leaders to be picked up and referenced over the course of your leadership journey.

Molly Langenstein, CEO and President, Chico's FAS

I've often told team members that if I seem like I have the answers, it's because I've just made most of the mistakes already. What excites me about ***Arrive. Drive. Thrive.™*** is the opportunity for emerging and aspiring managers to avoid those mistakes by putting its recommendations into practice. With structured exercises, templates and action plans for each major concept, this book answers the "how do you do that" question that so many business books fail to address. Highly recommended!

Paul Pickard, Chief Technology Officer, Korrus

I thoroughly loved reading ***Arrive. Drive. Thrive.™*** because it focuses on empowering leadership for emerging leaders. It is written in the most personable manner with such ease and flow. The personal examples shared led to a deeper and more effective understanding of all the important concepts raised in the book. The thought starters really helped to evoke deeper thinking and provide a framework for action versus leaving the concepts in the ethereal space. I loved the booster concepts as they are filled with important reminders and lessons.

Natalie Spiro, CEO/Founder, Blue Fire Leadership and Rhythm Agenda

Arrive. Drive. Thrive.™ is a thoughtful book taking you through the self discovery of leadership. The easy to use tools that accompany every chapter allow all levels of management to take time for an introspective look at what makes them tick and how to improve on themselves and their processes. [My firm] ALT HR Partners will be recommending this book to first time managers, as well as experienced managers who are working to find their way.

Shawn Straub, MA, SPHR, SHRM-SCP, Owner ALT HR Partners

A practical and actionable guide for those who desire to grow as leaders within their business and community. ***Arrive. Drive. Thrive.™***, like a toolbelt, has tactical advice for situations that managers and leaders encounter as they navigate within a company. For those that aspire to grow and lead within their organizations, I highly recommend this book.

Brad Miller, Vice President of International Sales, Hooker Furniture

Arrive. Drive. Thrive.™ is an exceptional book for leaders at all levels. This book is a great primer for aspiring leaders, a guide for emerging leaders, and a wonderful resource for senior leaders. I love how Josh, Nettie, and Gerald take you on the journey from Arriving to Driving to Thriving in your role and along the way help you unlock and recognize your full potential as a leader.

Susan A. Miele, PhD, Chief People Officer, Ginkgo Bioworks, Inc.

Practical, challenging, yet encouraging. If you are a business leader, have leadership responsibilities, or just want to become a great leader, then ***Arrive. Drive. Thrive.™*** can help you transition not only yourself, it can help you transform your company, and more importantly, your future.

Scott Pharr, President, Piedmont Truck Center

This book provides a roadmap for anyone in a leadership or management position seeking to enhance their abilities. Oftentimes roadmaps provide clear direction but sometimes fall flat on the "why". As a result many struggle to tie the roadmap to their own careers and businesses. ***Arrive. Drive. Thrive.™*** provides a clear, succinct way to not only approach leadership but also how to manifest those skills successfully in business; in short it ties the HOW directly to the WHY.

I am often seeking new materials to share with my management students. This book will provide a structured guide for my students that will help build upon the skills they learn in my classroom. Further this book will emphasize, for my students, the importance of developing leadership and management skills. These skills will help them in their careers to support the needs of their organizations. I am excited to utilize this book in future classes.

Kelly Colón, Director of Workplace Strategy, Cresa; Adjunct Professor, Wentworth College

I love ***Arrive. Drive. Thrive.™*** because it encourages development throughout one's career and creates the mindset that it is okay to continue learning. When it comes to leading a team, I believe the concept of understanding from your team's perspective is remarkably important to truly be an effective leader. My biggest takeaway from the book is that leadership is a constant work in progress; and that is okay, as the journey is filled with tremendous learning opportunities.

Jonathan A. Autry, Assistant Vice President and Branch Manager, First National Bank Corporation

Arrive. Drive. Thrive.™ covers a lot of ground touching on all aspects of leadership while providing a roadmap for new and emerging leaders. All new leaders would benefit from the helpful topics, tools, tips, and insights provided. A unique resource in this book is the "Booster Concepts". Years of leadership and coaching experience went into providing guidance into specific actions you can take to develop each aspect of your leadership. Whenever faced with a new challenge or situation, pull out this book for practical and useful guidance and resources at any point along your leadership journey.

Liz Fitzgerald, President, XChange Consulting, Inc.

I had the great honor of reading a preview of ***Arrive. Drive. Thrive.™*** for aspiring, emerging, and growing leaders. I have also had the honor of working closely with two of the authors Gerald Hutchinson, as my executive coach, and Josh Saterman as a co-executive at Macy's, Inc., and now a strategic business partner and fellow consultant for Rodan and Fields.

The authors clearly pour their years of experience and wisdom into a blueprint for successful navigation through the stages of leadership.

What I love most about ***Arrive. Drive. Thrive.™*** is it recognizes that everyone is on a unique leadership journey, they have their own stories, and diverse backgrounds that help to shape the leader they will become.

Arrive. Drive. Thrive.™ is a must read for anyone looking to grow as a leader. It is a recipe for living a profound, fulfilling, and meaningful life — so you can leave your personal mark to make a positive impact on the world.

Taran Chernin, former retail C-suite executive, and current Level V Circle Executive Consultant, Rodan and Fields

Dedication

To all our clients who have taught us patience, compassion, and humility.

...

To Josh's grandfather, Jack Stateman, for always being my friend.

To Becky Dannenfelser, for always being a guiding light.

To my father, Gerald Sr., for his insightful intelligence and lessons about confidentiality.

To Jimmy Kausch, with whom I drank many glasses of Scotch and laughed about the absurdity of life in organizations.

To Nettie's grandparents, Sam and Tibey who shared their love, wisdom, and knowledge with their grandchildren.

To Nettie's parents, Paul and Hedria, who taught me how to connect with people, work hard, have fun, and be a mensch.

...

Your lessons and memories live on within us and within this book. We love and appreciate you.

Personal Gratitudes

To our colleagues, peers, mentors, and sponsors for always being our strength when we needed you the most.

We could not have completed this book without the unbelievable support of our loved ones and community colleagues. Their love, encouragement, thought partnership, and genuine joy for us gave tenacity, drive, and courage.

- *Michael Saterman, Husband and COO, Managing Partner, Saterman Connect*
- *Michelle Ostroff, Culture and Office Connector, Saterman Connect*
- *Jed, Perri, and Kayla Nitzberg, Husband and Daughters*
- *Leslie Kausch and Daniel Hutchinson-Kausch, Wife and Son*

Professional Gratitudes

Alphagraphics Duluth | Johns Creek, Duluth, GA, www.alphagraphicsdjc.com

Bill Gentner, president and owner, AlphaGraphics Duluth Johns Creek, a marketing and printing firm in Atlanta that helps clients present the best version of their brand. A former CMO and marketing executive, he's is passionate for helping clients grow their business.

Publify Relations, USA, www.publifyrelations.com

Sarah Solomon, the founder of Publify Relations specializes in working with clients within the Business/Leadership and Diversity, Equity, and Inclusion industries. She has helped many of her clients with successful book launches garnering quality media buzz and attention.

Studio29, Manchester, United Kingdom, www.studio29design.co.uk

Lee Potts and Ste (Stephen) Luckett head up Studio29 Design, a global full-service creative agency that combines strategy and design to help bring people and brands together.

DiCaprio.Consulting, New York, NY, peter@dicaprio.consulting

Peter DiCaprio is the founder of DiCaprio.Consulting, helping organizations enhance profitability and equity through coaching, organizational development, and training. Much of his work emphasizes diminishing the impact of bias on decision making.

TABLE OF CONTENTS

ARRIVE. DRIVE. THRIVE.

For Aspiring, Emerging, and Growing Leaders

EMPOWER YOUR LEADERSHIP

GERALD HUTCHINSON Ph.D.

NETTIE NITZBERG M.Ed.

JOSHUA SATERMAN

PREFACE

Some people aspire to run marathons. Other people dream of winning that championship. Each person has a goal, a dream, something that makes them sing. One of our dreams was to write a book together. We wanted to share our experiences as managers, leaders, bosses, colleagues, teammates, supervisors, direct reports, friends, mentors, sponsors, advocates, consultants, and most importantly, as fellow human beings. We've had both personal and professional adventures; those have created stories that we believe can help other humans on their journey.

We learn about ourselves through experiencing other people's stories. We found wisdom can be realized through storytelling. Stories stick with us. Each of us can think back to those individuals and experiences that have impacted our journeys. Even more fascinating, sometimes hearing the same story or stories repeatedly at different moments in your life will continue to impact you.

Josh's Story: How We Influence One Another

> *A great example of this is your grandparents or senior members of your family sharing with you a story. My grandfather used to ride the tilt-a-whirl ride at amusement parks with the biggest smile. He*

> *was in his late seventies and had a heart condition. I remember my family saying that these rides were too big a risk for my grandfather. I also remember thinking, "he's fine and he's young at heart". Now, as I look back on this story it has a new meaning. The same story might have impacted you in different ways depending on where you heard the story in your life's journey.*
>
> *Grandpa knew that smiling was the best medicine. I knew that it brought him joy and that memory now withstands the test of time. Grandpa also knew that Grandma would never let him explore that ride without me riding with him. In some ways, he used me, his grandson, for good reasons, to experience joy for himself. He knew there was strength in numbers and that alone was never as fun as together. Perhaps this was a luxury his family couldn't afford growing up or my grandparents wouldn't tackle such a feat like riding an amusement ride. My grandfather didn't want to be that grandfather. He wanted to take that calculated risk.*
>
> *His influence on me and my own development has inspired me to ask Gerald and Nettie to write this book with me so we can together inspire, motivate, and empower you to smile while becoming the great leader you are capable of becoming.*

Now let's consider this personal story in a workplace context. Think back to stories your mentor or a senior leader might have shared with you. Consider how these moments and experiences have influenced you. Little details matter as they paint your career path. Our goal is that this book — in sharing stories, information, observations and more — will provide guidance and helpful pathways for you to consider as you influence others. We want to help you gain insight on topics such as:

- How do you prepare to welcome a new teammate?
- What will you do and say to your new hire to share your vision, your successes, and help them become part of the culture?
- What are the legacies you wish to leave your organization, your team, your direct reports?
- In what ways are the actions of each day creating 'mentor moments' for people in your lives?

One of the best parts of any adventure is the anticipation of beginning your journey. Our hope is to help your journey along the way. This book is essential for leaders who are new in their journey. It's also great for leaders who want to inspire new leaders on their internal and extended teams. It's also built to be revisited.

We want this book to serve as a 'tool' that you can keep returning to and, like a well-told story, continue to find more meaning and connection as you build your career and continue your journey.

What do we mean by *ARRIVE*?

ARRIVE means becoming prepared to lead. You learn more about who you are as a leader. You learn about your role and responsibilities, and the path of your individual leadership journey.

Knowing what it takes to lead accelerates your ability to build a team, and to get things done. Those who are not prepared typically flounder in their early stages of leadership, and often learn the hard way, if at all. Those who are prepared will do better when they arrive at the first steps of their journey.

What do we mean by *DRIVE*?

DRIVE is all about achieving results from and with your team. Results that are impactful. Results that serve the organization, and results that move the organization forward in a significant manner.

There will inevitably be some experimentation. Some uncertainty. Some moving backward, and even sideways. Success in business is almost never a straight line forward and upward.

When you ***DRIVE***, you know how to make good things happen, using your team as the conduit to success … even if your organization is not entirely sure how to coordinate greater outcomes. By using the principles, tools, and tactics in this book, you will have confidence that those good things will happen.

What do we mean by *THRIVE*?

It's not enough just to drive and get results. We want you to Thrive, be on top of your game. To not just have more wins than losses, but to have a winning season. To get into the playoffs. Maybe win a championship. When you DRIVE, you are better positioned to ***THRIVE***.

Introduction

ARRIVE. DRIVE. THRIVE.™

What is Leadership?

Leadership is Influence: *Influencing others to think, feel, or act differently than they might on their own.* Every time you see the word "leadership" in this book or hear it uttered by others, you should immediately think "influence."

When you see leadership from this perspective, you will see leadership all around you: in simple efforts and complicated ones, in virtuous ones, and corrupt ones. Sometimes inspired and transformational, such as getting you to accept a whole new way of behaving, and sometimes mundane, such as getting you to file your reports on time.

Leadership is an incredibly complex and dynamic subject. Whole libraries are devoted to the subject. Yet complexity is the enemy of comprehension. So, be patient with yourself and others while you build your leadership from the tools we provide in this book which is designed to empower aspiring, emerging, and growing leaders.

Let's start by laying out some of the framework of leadership. Later, we'll get into the "how to." For just a bit, let's step back and consider a few key points that put the leadership challenge into perspective.

1. *People Need Leadership*

   Even leaders need leaders who can support them to see situations from different perspectives, or see further into the future, or see aspects that may be hidden. People need a vision. They need a mission, something bigger than themselves that they can attach to and help create, and to put their effort into in order to make things better. While you may be fortunate to have such people on your team already, that sense of vision; and mission, of zeal to throw action into achieving a goal, can also decrease over time. Even if you have super-motivated team members, they may not be organized to coordinate their efforts in a coherent way to achieve big things. People need concrete goals, and someone who can structure and sequence their actions to achieve those bigger goals.

   The wise leader doesn't have to be The Leader. But they have to be willing to nudge and guide and shape and structure things so that good things happen. They can share leadership, handing off the baton of direction to others when appropriate. Just make sure that if you are the designated leader, that you are careful and discerning when you let someone else step up and lead your team so that they can be successful and lead with their strengths.

2. *You Can Be a Leader Without Being a Manager*
   You might be a subject matter expert with zero direct reports. You can still consider yourself a leader and support your organization moving forward through the power of influence. The initiatives of a leader often involve the use of a variety tools to influence others to accomplish needed goals. You might need to use your ability to manage a project, or your authority as an expert, or your ability to evoke other's emotions (passions) to influence others to get the job done.

   You are the initiator, and you can only lead to the capacity or skill level that you have attained. Work to grow. Your growth as a leader is essential.

3. *Leaders Serve the Highest Principle*
   Leaders must stay true to the 'Highest Principle'– productive contribution to the business. The Highest Principle is the most stable point of reference. It is like the North Star for sailors seeking direction in the middle of the ocean. It should be the constant against which all other options are considered.

   Sometimes leaders must make a stand against what they see as disruption to the Highest Principle. This often feels (and *is*) risky, and if they have fidelity to the Highest Principle, they will find the courage that is associated with that faithfulness.

4. *Leadership is Simple, but it is Not Simplistic*
   Human behavior can seem to be completely odd, illogical, nonsensical, and overly complex. Yet, once you

can discern the pattern of human dynamics, the logic is easy to understand. It becomes much easier to influence others.

There are simple actions and behaviors that work well for leading others that we will discuss in this book. This is the simple part. But we see leadership as being like a kaleidoscope: turn the tube just a little bit, and the entire pattern changes. And because things change -- both on the outside in the working situation, as well as "inside" each person -- the leader has to be constantly aware and willing to shift, evolve, and adapt their way of influencing. Therefore, leadership is not simplistic.

In a kaleidoscope of people, interests, abilities, motivations, and agendas, situations that on the surface look similar, may be very different. What works in one situation may not work so well in another. And that leads us to point number 5.

5. *Leadership is a Moving Target*
   As Heraclitus once said, "No person ever steps into the same river twice, for it's not the same river, and they are not the same person." Things change all the time. The conditions in which leaders operate constantly changes. The marketplace changes. Technology changes. And workforce and workplace change. People's motivations change and their fears change. People change their capabilities, their interests, and their rituals. Leaders must be agile, flexible, and committed to continuous learning about the craft of leadership. The art and science of leadership requires a lifetime of study. Every day, because each day is different, the leader is provided with opportunities to flex and grow.

But that does not mean leadership is ambiguous. On the contrary, the great variety of experiences cries for greater stability at a deeper level so that people are not tossed about by the storms of change. The leader who understands this need can maintain integrity to the course of progress, while flexing with the ebb and flow of the various currents that may seek to sweep the ship onto a rocky shore.

6. *Each Individual is Different, so Lead with Your Authentic Self*
   Just as no two individuals are alike, no two leaders are alike. You bring your unique perspectives, strengths, weaknesses, background, vision, dreams, frustrations, good habits, bad habits, ethics, attitude, and evolving maturity to your role. Sometimes you will be able to follow the suggestions of other leaders, and model yourself effectively after them. Sometimes, you will want to act like a certain leader and find that style of leadership does not feel comfortable for you. That's ok. You've got to lead from where you are.

   Leading with your authentic self is a balancing act between your own comfort, and the demands of the situation. For instance, you may have strength in creating harmony with others, and the situation demands that you act fast and decisively, potentially creating some upset feelings. You will have to wrap the need for that fast decision in the velvet glove of harmony. This takes some finesse and can be done. Therefore, being a leader is all about balancing the art and the science of leadership.

7. *Multiple Ways to Influence*
   Since leadership is about influence, let's understand the

five main levers of influencing others that you can have in an organization:

1. *Management - structuring of people, activity, and resources to get things done*
2. *Authority - using power of position or expertise to command the actions of others*
3. *Reason - using logic to convince others to act in a desirable way*
4. *Emotion - evoking an emotional experience to motivate others to perform*
5. *Social pressure - using the desire to fit in and be one of the groups to provoke action*

All these levers can be used singly or in combination, and all may be effective. In part, their effectiveness will depend on the skill of the leader wielding them, as well as the match between the tactics, the situation, and the audience. Good leadership (are you thinking "influence?") is like finding the right key to unlock the understanding, motivation, and action of others. It is dialing these methods up or down, as needed. Use them, and watch and learn how effective your technique is, so that you can continually grow in your ability to influence.

8. *Integrity is Everything*
   Finally, wise leaders are careful to act with integrity in everything they do. They realize that if they intentionally misrepresent the facts, if they don't do what they say they will, if they are unfaithful or untrustworthy, then they ultimately have nothing. They lose credibility. They have become un-*believe*-able. It is not always easy to tell the

truth, and not always easy to deliver what you say you will. But it is a heavy lift to get your integrity back, once lost. Leaders know that being vulnerable and making mistakes are okay. We are humans. We can all make mistakes if those mistakes are not intentional. Great leaders seek forgiveness, learn from their experiences, and move forward, as they err, maintaining their integrity.

SUMMARY: Good leadership requires that you engage in a continual process of learning about how to be more influential, well as how and when to step back and let others influence you. We say with 100% certainty that the more you grow as a person, the more that you seek to understand others, and how to educate, motivate, and hold them accountable, the better you will become as a leader. It is a lifelong journey.

Section 1

ARRIVE.

Preparing for Your Success

1
Arriving as a Leader

I have learned that success is to be measured not so much by the position that one has reached in life as by the obstacles which he has had to overcome while trying to succeed.

Booker T. Washington

Your Leadership Platform

Where you lead from comes from who you are. Your talents, skills and competencies, values, habits, personality, biases, beliefs---all these are the "platform" from which you lead yourself and others. Some are powerful and highly useful, some do not make a difference one way or the other, and some may be like trash in your head that hinders effective performance and leadership. So, it is important to know your platform. NOTE: It will change as you learn and grow.

The philosopher Will Durant summarized the thoughts of Aristotle as, *"We are what we repeatedly do. Excellence then, is not an act, but a habit."* We say it more simply: ***Success is a habit, not an event.***

The creation of success is your goal. Success breeds more success for you and your organization. Let's consider the sequence of events that will get you and your team from here (arrive) to there (thrive). You have got to know...

- Where you want to go.
- What resources you've got to work with.
- How to make a plan.
- How to motivate others to help you get there (and since you are a leader, you'll want others to get there with you, since getting there yourself but leaving others behind is simply selfish).
- Ways to execute that plan.
- When evaluating your progress in achieving your goals, first look at acutal success, then in terms of the process of getting to the goal...so that you can ultimately do better next time.

To develop the habit of success, focus on these factors with intention, be willing to constantly learn, and continually work on getting better every day.

There are three phases to get there: Arrive. Drive. and **Thrive.**

For each phase of the journey, **Arrive. Drive.** and **Thrive.,** past influences and future desires come together shaping your thinking, decisions, and behavior. Simply put, you will lead in part from your experience, and in part from the wisdom of the experiences of others. The 26-year-old Marine working as a Store Security Lead will think differently based on their past experiences than a 26-year-old Store Manager who majored in Marketing at a small college. Likewise, each of their decisions will be shaped by their expectations and vision for the future for themself, their team, and their organization.

Your own past experiences and future desires shape your approach to life. You are where you are because of your past leading up to this moment. This affects where you wish to go in the future, and the actual things you do today, tomorrow, and day-by-day to create that future.

We call this mix of past influences and future aspirations your **Platform**. It is the foundation of your decisions that lead to your actions. If you wish to lead with wisdom and purposefulness, then it is essential to grasp the impact that your Platform exerts on how you decide to act.

> ***"Who are you?" I asked.***
>
> *"Who am I?" my client repeated. "What do you mean? I have my role here as manager. I have my college degree. I have my history of success. I've charted my course to get here, and here is looking pretty good!"*
>
> ***"Yes," I replied. "Those are all real. And they have value to you, and to some others. But the meaning that others attach to those components may just get in your way...or they may also support you! "***
>
> *"I'm not sure I follow."*
>
> ***"Well, there are limits to how much you can define yourself."***
>
> *"Really?! Tell me more," my client asked.*
>
> ***"Look at it this way: You graduated from a state university. It may be considered one of the public "Ivies" and a degree to be proud of, but someone who graduated from Harvard or Stanford will always think that they one-up you in terms of status. On the other hand, many people think of those who graduated from an Ivy League school as arrogant***

elitists who only have a credential. Just as those who graduated from a community college may think of you as a credential arrogant elitist with your fancy degree from the flagship state university."

"I think I'm starting to see what you mean," my client said.

"So, you can see that the meaning they attach to what you show them will be shaped by their own background and experience."

"Oh yeah! Big time!"

"Let's take it one step further. What you think of yourself can be positive and negative. You put out a vibe based upon what you think of yourself and conveying that message to others. They may not be able to describe it, but they can feel it, and attach meaning to it.

"OK, now you're starting to trouble me!"

"Good. That means you are on the verge of learning!"

"And what am I to learn today, Coach?!"

"You lead from your personal platform, but your platform is not a static entity. It constantly grows taking on new shapes, just as an acorn grows into an oak. The acorn's growth is impacted by the soil in which it takes root, the water, nutrients, and sunlight it gets, and the extremes of the seasons. The environment influences the growth of the oak, just as your environment influences and changes you.

"So, your platform is not just the tangibles of your past. That is evidence of where you have been. The

> ***intangibles are just as important—your character, your personality strengths, your values—these define how you make decisions just as surely as your track record has impacted what you have learned. Your roots and the things that nourish you, these impact your personal platform."***
>
> *"I'm starting to see what you mean."*
>
> **"Good. Knowing that your platform is the only place that you can lead from, you may want to make sure it is solid, and not built on quicksand. For those whose platforms have no integrity, are not leaders, but are functionaries with power, also known as petty tyrants in service to their masters, and they have no soul."**
>
> *"I've known a few of those!"*
>
> **"As have we all. Don't be a petty tyrant. Build your leadership grounded in virtue, with a solid and reliable platform, and you will do well in life."**
>
> *"How do I start?"*
>
> **"Study yourself! This was the way of the ancients, and it is the way of the future."**

Are you aware of the following factors that are planks in your Leadership Platform?

1. Your "Why" or Purpose
2. Your Personality
3. Your Character
4. Your Strengths
5. Your Values

6. Your Skill Set and Expertise
7. Your Track Record
8. Your Critical "Lessons Learned"
9. Your Vision

Let us look at each one of these planks as you **ARRIVE.** You may not be able to intentionally use these influences at all times; however, it is important to do an audit from time to time to understand the foundation and framework from which you lead.

It is never too late to be what you might have been.

George Eliot

1: Your "Why"

There is a profound difference in performance, motivation, and inspiration between the brick-mason who is laying bricks to make a wage, and the brick-mason who is building a monument. Their "Why" is different. Who would you rather work next to? Who enjoys their work more, no matter the hardship? Who is more inspiring to you, to elevate appreciation for your own work?

What is your deeper motivation or purpose for working, and for choosing this particular job with this particular company?

Simon Sinek, the business philosopher, has said that the best companies begin with understanding their "Why." Why are they in this business? What do they do? How do they do it? In what ways are they servants to their Why? And this makes sense. Likewise, if you really are clear on your personal "Why" (your purpose, your motivation), then it becomes much easier to lead and inspire others.

Taking this into perspective, your personal "Why" can start small and grow.

> ***"Why" Matters, by Gerald Hutchinson***
>
> *My first job out of college was managing a sporting goods retailer basing my "Why" on making money and enjoying an active, adventurous lifestyle. Purely self-centered.*
>
> *I did not really know my "Why" until I was about 28 years old, when I finally realized that my "Why" is to help others learn more about the world, themselves, and their options so that they could make better decisions and lead a better life. At the time I accomplished that through selling outdoor adventure gear and clothing, helping my customers have more satisfying and fulfilling outdoor experiences. Then I fulfilled my "why" through leading others on wilderness adventures in the Appalachian Mountains and the Everglades in Florida. My "Why" was helping my students learn more about leadership, teamwork, and themselves. As my "Why" grew into coaching and consulting business leaders, I recognized that this gave me more leverage. If they became better leaders, then they would influence their employees to be better people.*
>
> *Be wary of what you are casting as your "Why". Have a grain of cynicism and be willing to question your own certainty of the righteousness of your "Why". History tells us that individuals, tribes, and societies have held opinions of self-righteous and absolute*

> *certainty that have been incredibly flawed and have led to misery and tragedy. People fool themselves all the time and rationalize dehumanizing others all too easily. If you believe that cannot happen to you, then call one of us, and we will have a discussion.*

BOOSTER CONCEPT

You can skip this step of writing down your "Why" ... however, your life will be more powerful, meaningful, and successful if you know your "Why" and are purposefully and intentionally taking steps to fulfill it.

THOUGHT STARTERS

- What do you want your story to be?
- How will your "Why" guide you today? Over the next 90 days?
- In what ways can your values and strengths serve you? In what ways are they holding you back?

2. Your Personality

What are the deeper patterns that influence your behavior? Most conclude those patterns come from your personality. Insight into your personality --- also known as self-awareness --- is powerful for a leader. Have you wondered where this personality comes from? The answer is: it depends. Neuroscience is contributing greater depth into this complex story and finding that some personality attributes such as "Agreeableness," could have a greater origin from your experiences in childhood ("nurture"), than other attributes such as IQ, which comes from your genetic inheritance from your biological parents (that is, "nature"). Nature or nurture in origin matters little. This is because both psychological research and this book's focus is on empowering your leadership.

What we are more concerned with is what you do with what you've got.

Psychological studies indicate that there are five major aspects to personality, which might be remembered with the acronym OCEAN:

- *Openness to Experience* (curiosity and imagination)
- *Conscientiousness* (being organized, productive, taking responsibility)
- *Extraversion* (sociability and social assertiveness)
- *Agreeableness* (showing friendliness and compassion toward others)
- *Neuroticism / Emotionality* (being more emotional about life circumstances, especially with tendencies towards anxiety and/or depression)

Some personality traits seem to be rather persistent through adulthood, while others are not quite as solidly set. For instance, the Agreeableness trait is more easily shaped and refined with age through socialization (see: Srivastava S, John OP, Gosling SD, Potter J (May 2003). "Development of personality in early and middle adulthood: set like plaster or persistent change?". *Journal of Personality and Social Psychology*. 84 (5): 1041–53).

While it is useful to gain awareness of your own inner "operating system," what is perhaps more important for a leader is to understand that not everyone sees the world as you do or is internally motivated in the same way. This insight is crucial to the effective use of your Platform.

Many different personality types can be successful in each role, though it's clear that some personality types may not be well-suited for success in certain roles. For instance, someone with low impulse-control will likely do poorly in positions requiring them to stay focused hour after hour, day after day, week after week.

After having coached thousands of managers in the last two decades, it is clear to us that three special points about personality are essential to keep in mind:

1. Your personality is only part of who you are. It does establish a pattern of processing information about you in your world and acting on that process. We can call those routines your comfort zone. You can expand your comfort zone if you take action that makes you uncomfortable, such as forcing yourself to speak in public even if you are shy or introverted or buckling down and doing detailed work if you are a generalist. While it is unlikely you will become an expert at these things beyond your comfort zone, don't underestimate yourself. Your beliefs about who you are and what you are capable of could be self-limiting. Learn to "flex" your habits and patterns to many more options on handling situations and challenges.
2. There is a side to each of us that is insecure, hurt, selfish, and untrusting and this aspect is hidden underneath layers of socialization that we use to do good things, positive things, productive things and thereby enjoy positive outcomes. Sometimes, our negativity leaks out and can sabotage our good intentions. We all seek to compensate for insecurity, self-doubt, or self-negativity through positive action which we use to prove "success." That compensation can also become over-compensation if it is a rigid, unyielding way of thinking and acting that can undermine agile, flexible, and on-purpose action. Watch out for it.

3. While "how you act" is dependent on who you are with and the situation, all things being equal, you will follow patterns of behavior arising from your personality. Some patterns will tend to prevail. Know what those patterns are so you can bring consciousness and purposefulness to your behavior and expand your repertoire of behavior; hence, expanding your "comfort zone." For instance, if you are an anxious person who tends to avoid risks, you will likely avoid many risks and seek to structure your environment so that you do not have to experience much anxiety. Yet, this may also mean that you miss out on opportunities. "If all you have is a hammer, you tend to see every problem as a nail." By expanding your toolbox with self-awareness, and a willingness to challenge your personality patterns you can increase your ability to effectively handle a wider range of situations and opportunities.

BOOSTER CONCEPT

Your personality may cause you to be unsatisfied with the current situation, and if you do not take concrete and often uncomfortable action to overcome it, then you'll just get more of the same. You've got to actually do something --- lots of 'things' --- to succeed at a high level. Action is a choice, not something destined by your personality. Action comes from your ability to reason and to put time and energy into a problem. Nurture your ability to operate outside your comfort zone.

THOUGHT STARTERS

- Describe a time when you were uncomfortable yet pushed through to accomplish something great.
- What did you learn about yourself and your ability to learn?

3. Your Character

Who have you made yourself to be? You are strongly influenced by your personality and your childhood influences in ways that may be difficult to alter over your lifespan. But your character is formed by the decisions that you make, the actions that you take, and the resulting conclusions you make about yourself and the proper way to act. These conclusions become new information about other decisions, and other actions. Repeated often enough, they form an identity that can be called your character. This includes your work-ethic---how hard you are willing to work.

NOTE: A more thorough discussion of crucial character attributes for your identity as a leader of others are developed more extensively in this chapter.

BOOSTER CONCEPT

Work to develop your character with virtue, not as a victim. Your character is an enduring tool for your work in the world and your ability to fulfill your "Why." Realize that you will fall down sometimes or be tempted to do things "out of character." Develop a core team of coaches, advisors, guides, and peers to help you to sustain your character when you are challenged, and to grow your character, always.

THOUGHT STARTER

- How would someone else describe your character? Have you ever considered asking your closest advocates that question?

4. Your Strengths

The way that we use the term "strengths" is in reference to the talents or aptitudes in which you are unconsciously good (see the ***Strengths & Talents*** section in this chapter). In other words, you do these things well without any struggle, and without even having to think about how you do it. Knowledge of your strengths allows you to position yourself to do tasks that are simply very easy, and you might not even experience performing those tasks as "work."

NOTE: A discussion of strengths is developed more extensively later in this chapter.

BOOSTER CONCEPT
Play to your strengths, as this gives you maximum leverage. Find workarounds for your weaknesses. Let others put their strengths to work to help you: get someone else who is strong where you are weak to do those tasks that are a challenge for you.

THOUGHT STARTER

- Describe your superpowers. List 2 or 3 strengths that you do better than anyone else. How do you know these are your superpowers?

5. Your Values

What really matters to you? Values can be thought of as emotional shortcuts that get to the things that you have learned to care about. So, when we say that someone values honesty, we can understand that they have come to believe that honesty is the best way to achieve their goals by creating stable, sustainable relationships built on mutual trust and free of conflict and violence. To illustrate the point by drawing a contrast---there are those persons who do not value honesty, and who value deceit. They are just as willing to lie as to tell the truth because they see deceit as a better way to get what they want than honesty. Those people have a very short time and fail to see the damage to their integrity and relationships when people find out they are untrustworthy.

In the professional world several values are common and all orient to the bottom-line of being productive and socially responsible---however that may be defined. You may have some differences in the degree to which you are motivated to align with those values, and you may have some values that are largely independent-of or irrelevant-to your corporate employer.

For instance, some people greatly value the beauty of their surroundings; some corporations consider aesthetics a trivial nuisance. A clash of values will likely produce an ill-fit between the individual and the organization, unless there are other important values that tilt the overall balance in a favorable direction.

BOOSTER CONCEPT
Humans are incredibly adaptable when it comes to values. For instance, across the globe, humans adopt very different cultural values, and then may adapt to somewhat contrary values when they move to foreign countries. Point being this: be aware of the values you are adopting, as they can help or hinder you in the fulfillment of your "Why."

THOUGHT STARTER

- When are you the most adaptable? Consider a time when adaptability served you or supported a decision you needed to make. Why?

6. Your Skill Sets and Expertise

In what activities have you developed skillful capability? You cannot be skilled or an expert in everything. You bring varying degrees of skill and expertise to your work. Fortunately, the beauty of modern civilization is that we can specialize in our skills and expertise. We can allow others to to specialize in skills that we don't possess.

It is natural to begin to see the world through the skill set or expertise-bias that each of us has. We use our skills and expertise as filtering mechanisms to think through our work challenges. That can be something of a mistake as it can trap us in our own limited perspective. Seeing the world through the expertise of others can support us to approach problems with new insight.

BOOSTER CONCEPT
Keep learning; always. One of the hallmarks of a great leader is their capacity to keep learning with an open mind. Never stop working to sharpen and extend your skill sets and expertise. Just small increments build up. For instance, if you want to stay on the sharp edge by reading more business books, you can easily read about 20 books a year by reading just 10 pages a day. Since the average business book is 180 pages long, you will finish in 18 days. 365 days divided by 18 = 20.2.

THOUGHT STARTERS

- What inspires you about your craft or perhaps your role as a leader?
- What do you want to learn next?

7. Your Track Record

What is your track record of accomplishments, blunders, and failures? Think of this as your *story*, and let's note that not all chapters or scenes in your story are created equal. The things that you tell yourself about your track record are in some ways more powerful than what you have done. For good or for ill.

Gerald worked with one senior manager who, early in his career, always seemed to be kicking off some initiative that held great promise of returns to his company. But before the results of that initiative were in, he always seemed to leave for another promotion at another company. Finally, as he got into his late middle age as an executive, his first bright initiative at his new position failed to produce the promised effect. Neither did the second, and since it was so costly, he got terminated. He was crushed because he thought he was a perennial winner. As he found out later, his supposedly brilliant early-career initiatives never bore fruit either. His track record looked like success to him and to those he was pitching himself to, and only because the results were never included.

Be aware that your blunders and so-so results have great teaching power for you. You should cherish them. We guarantee that you will learn ten times more from a failure than from a brilliant success!

BOOSTER CONCEPT:
Feel proud of your honest successes. Commit to bite-size goals that you can accomplish, and ensure you are reaching nonetheless. And be humble; make sure you give credit to those who also contributed, for no one succeeds anymore without the work of others. (Someone who hogs the spotlight, or steals ideas or credit from others, makes enemies. That's bad, okay? Don't do it.)

THOUGHT STARTERS

- What does success look like for you across the next 90 days? 1 year? 3-5 years?
- What does success for your team look like across the same 90 days? 1 year? 3-5 years?

8. Your Critical "Lessons Learned"

What are the events that have brought you insight and wisdom, and that get repeated in your mental conversation, or in the stories you tell yourself and about yourself? These often cycle through short mental phrasings: "Never go to a meeting without reviewing the roster." "Never leave a meeting without knowing who is doing what by when." "Make sure you know their partner's name." There can be hundreds. If you can, capture them in writing. They are useful direction-tellers.

BOOSTER CONCEPT

The smart person learns from their own experience; the wise person learns from the experience of others. Ask what others that have done worked, and what they've done that has NOT worked. And take heed of their examples.

THOUGHT STARTERS

- How do you share your story?
- How do you hold yourself accountable?

9. Your Vision

What are you trying to create in your role? What is your point of view? (And is it relevant to others?) Your vision is the way that you picture your destination. Imagine a sailing ship on the ocean. It can go in any direction, land at any port. What port do you wish to visit?

Having that image of a destination is powerful. Without it, you will not know which direction to head, or what to do to get there. You cannot plot out waypoints, or mile-markers to give you an idea of your progress to achieve that desired state.

The more clearly you can imagine that future state---really see it with your mind's eye---the more likely you will be to achieve it. But imagination itself is not enough to get you there. You must also make choices along the way about your priorities and set goals and practices that will get you there.

With whom are you sharing your vision? Consider an accountability partner(s), or trusted partner(s), that can share any gaps or blind spots that perhaps you might have missed.

BOOSTER CONCEPT
Talk about your vision with a professional certified coach to clarify and commit to it. Write it down, take pictures of it, spend time getting as many of your senses as possible involved. Make it real and set goals that will let you know you are achieving progress. And review your goal daily. A journey of a thousand miles takes many steps.

THOUGHT STARTERS

- Who are your accountability partners today?
- Who is going to hold you accountable?
- How are those accountability partners providing you feedback, and are you open to their feedback?

10. Your Personal Brand

Your Personal Brand is the impression that people form (in their emotional minds) when they think of you. Your Brand exists, therefore, as an emotional response by others, however subtle or however much they recognize that fact. Yet, it is an outgrowth of your history, and the things that you do. Consequently, your brand is a unique part of your platform, and may have a significant impact on your ability to get things done.

Logic and facts play only a small part in the brand impression that others get from you, due to several biases that they are largely unaware of.

Companies spend millions every year to shape your impression of them, and little of it has to do with the specific details of their product offerings. Their brand management is directly tied to manipulating your emotions when you think of them. You may find that you need to do some work to "buff up your brand" or to sustain it. You can shape the "brand" impressions and emotions about your own abilities, capabilities, and strengths. It takes intention and consistency. And if you are trying to create a brand impression that is beyond your genuine ability to improve, it can be exhausting!

Quite a few things make up the impression/brand that others derive from their experience with you. How can you leverage a trusted colleague who knows you well enough to support you understanding how you present yourself? Consider the following factors:

- The Quality of Your Thinking - your communication and other artifacts of your mind's work (such as PowerPoint slides, texts, papers, and e-mails.); the questions you ask; how you go about solving a problem; how much you reach out to others for their input; what "filters" you use for seeing a problem; the breadth or scope of the problems you see and work on; how essential that problem-solving is for real business needs; your insight; your analytical innovation process and output

- The Quality of Your Deliverables to Solve Identified Problems - observed through the breadth and depth of your solution, and the approach you used to get there.
- The Timeliness of your Deliverables - are they premature, on-time, late?
- The Pace of Your Productive Activity (Urgency) - observed by how often team meetings are held, how emphatic you are about achieving milestones, how rigorously you hold others to account for their productivity.
- Evidence of the Sequencing of Your Actions - the logic you use to organize your activity, and the effectiveness of that organization. Are you a "Ready, Aim, Fire" contributor, or a "Fire, Ready, Aim" contributor? Explore the 90-Day Individual Growth Plan (IGP) section for how you can be a smarter sequencer.
- The Clarity of Your Message – simpler is better. Work your key messages down to easily remembered words and not cliches. What others hear is not always what you said or intended to say. So, be intentional with how you say and reinforce your messages.
- The Consistency of Your Effort - the sense of purposefulness that you demonstrate. As a contrast, do you flit from one activity to another without sticking with something and really following through?
- The Durability of Your Results - how long do your improvement projects or other actions continue to add

value; how transformative are they, or do they nibble at margins; do your small efforts have compounding effects?

- Your Style in Social- and Business- Environments
  - Your Focus versus "Scatter-brained"
  - Your Confidence – self-assurance, poise, charisma, also known as "savoir faire" or handling of social situations you will face as a leader
  - Your Pacing - the match of your tempo to the agenda
  - Your Tone - the "song" of your voice
  - Your Point of View - self-focused versus other-focused
  - Loudness of Your Voice
  - Frequency of Utterances - chatty versus quiet
  - Physical Attributes and/or body language - face, posture, physique
  - Authenticity - observed as being "true to yourself"
  - Comfort with Others - expressed through the above bullets
  - Candor - how forthright and blunt you are
  - Narcissism - how much you focus on yourself
- Your Style in Communication - the tone and visual style of your memos, e-mails, voice mails such as seriousness/ mirthfulness; on-pointedness versus rambling; thoughtful-ness; comprehensiveness; articulateness; courteousness
- Your Grace Under Pressure - how you deal with stress, push-back from others, and conflict
- Your Work Story - biographical info; work history; significance of contributions; reputation; referrals from others

- Your Strengths, Talents, Skills, and Capabilities - these are the resources you bring to the table to accomplish activities and projects
- Your Achilles Heel or Blindspot (often Hidden) - this can be something that is missing, or it can be a strength that is overdone
- Your Dress - how are you dressing for an environment or situation
- Your Personal Space and Items - pictures in your workspace, laptop brand, stickers, water bottle, coffee cup, satchel/ backpack, other wearables, your virtual background
- Your Backstory – significant experiences that shaped and defined who you've become

BOOSTER CONCEPT

Conduct a Personal Brand Analysis with a friend or a trusted coach or advisor to help you understand your brand. Use the criteria listed above. This can be part of your Development Plan, whether overt or as a completely private element that does not get shared with others. Use the worksheet on the next page. A 360 Feedback Report and/or profile can be a useful tool to help you gain a better understanding of your brand, and how people around you can hold quite a range of opinions about you. In the end, there may be one defining facet to your personal brand that nullifies all others. Understand that part of what's great about being human is our ability to grow and remake ourselves. Everybody loves the story of one who did so!

THOUGHT STARTERS

- Which of these impressions speaks the most to you? How will you prioritize those impressions that you know are important, and previously didn't consider?

- Who within your organization or your professional circle demonstrates impressions that you desire to emulate and aspire to build into impressions you will be known for yourself?

Your Character as a Leader

[NOTE: This section on Character is the intellectual property of Gerald Hutchinson, Copyright © 2007-2021, and is published with the permission of the author.]

Character is the pattern of ***how you act*** in easy times and challenging times.

> *"What do you think we should do?" Jim, the CEO asked.*
>
> *He leaned back in his chair at the table with Sara, his client manager, and Paulo, the project manager of the build. They were reviewing the status of the project and realized that they had made a crucial error in the estimate they had given in the contract, and they were very likely not to make much of a profit, and if things did not run perfectly to the end, they could lose money.*
>
> *Sara said, "Well, we could assign it to the contingency fund. I think there may be enough to cover this error. It will cost the client more money, but they won't necessarily know it was our fault. They certainly accepted that risk when they signed the contract."*
>
> *"Hmmm," Jim said. He took a slow breath and rubbed his eyes.*
>
> *"Sara, I want to thank you for bringing this to my attention. You could have hidden this until we were*

submitting invoices further into the project. You did the right thing by letting me know as soon as you realized it." He turned towards Paulo.

"What is your take on this, Paulo?"

"Well, it is our mistake. We simply botched the estimate. I think we can cut some corners here and there in the remaining stages and probably scratch by with a little profit. I'm not sure that the client will be happy with that approach, as they did want a high-quality build, not just good-enough."

Jim looked at the two trusted employees who he had come to favor almost as his own children. They could tell he was resigned to a course of action that would not be easy.

"Alright guys. Here's what we are going to do, and why. I'm going to immediately call Carlos the owner. I'm going to tell him that we made a mistake, and that his building is going to cost an extra $80,000. I am going to tell him that this means that we will have to watch all remaining expenses with a microscope, and that even then we will be lucky to break even on this project. I am going to tell him that you two caught the mistake, and that we are fortunate that you did. We will see what he says at that point.

"Now, the reason that I am doing this is this: we made a deal, and we are sticking to that deal. It will be painful, and you know that without a profit, you will not be getting a performance bonus for this. But when I talk to Carlos, he will know that we do what we say we will do. He will know that we respect him and his opinion, and that part of that respect is being honest with him.

> *"You two have never made a mistake like this before. But everyone is human. No one has gotten hurt, except for our pocketbooks, and we can make that up perhaps some other time. We will have to be extremely disciplined for the remainder of the project. And I want you both to know that you are more valuable members of my team now than before. This is a lesson that we will not forget, and that we cannot forget.*
>
> *"I will look into other projects for how we might be able to recover some of this profit if you two are willing to be under greater scrutiny for a bit. I'd really like you to make more money. Let's use this situation to reinforce how important it is to be disciplined in our cost estimating process moving forward, as well as the importance of keeping your word. How does that sound?"*

In many ways, 'character' may be the most important acquired characteristic of a manager.

As a manager moves away from being a subject matter expert and moves into the role of strategic thinker and steward of the organization, who they are and what they stand for becomes ever more important. Being competent at technical or operational tasks is essential, and it doesn't set you apart from the crowd or make you a great leader.

Definition: Character is the composite of durable attributes that makes someone consistent in their actions in the world. Ideally, a leader's character is virtuous and thus capable of handling the challenges before them without regressing to unethical, illegal, rude, erratic, or merely pragmatic behavior. Character is acquired developmentally, from the interaction of the raw material of an individual's personality mixed with the reality of life experiences.

Character establishes the difference between the ordinary and the exceptional manager. If managers claim to have free will and the ability to make choices, then they must also accept the obligations of building and sustaining their character if they wish to be anything more than a leader based on position, power, or title.

Nothing reveals character more than adversity. And it will often reveal that the individual who thought they were bullet-proof lacks character in important ways.

That said, let's be real: maintaining good character in times of uncertainty and pressure is difficult. And this is where a team is important. Teammates can help one another maintain their character and avoid weakening and yielding to pragmatism or worse when the strain and pressure of challenges bears down.

Baseline Character Attributes for a Professional

Before an employee can be a good manager, they must be a solid professional, possessing a baseline of professional character attributes. The eight-character attributes listed below are timeless because they are essential for a professional contributor. There are an additional four-character attributes that support transforming a meaningful contributor into a best-in-class leader.

Remember that it is unlikely that someone will be "perfect" in these character attributes. Practicing good character is like practicing good habits: the more you do them, the more you can rely on them without even thinking about it. Aristotle spoke to the concept that success is not a single event, but a persistence of habit is doing the right things over and over and over, as it is with character too. One episode of good character will not make up for a pattern of poor character behaviors. Thus, to be able to claim good character, practice it relentlessly.

NOTE: Some character traits noted by other authors are likely embedded within the ones here, such as "Honesty" which is embedded into "Integrity." This is to make the list concise and compact.

1. **Integrity:** Professionals do what they say they will do. They are honest and do not lie. They act with high ethical and legal standards. They earn and maintain the trust of others through the integrity of their actions, for they know that once trust is lost, it is practically impossible to reclaim it.
2. **Respect:** Professionals respect others' differences, even while they may not agree with or believe in the value of those differences. They show respect for traditions even while they may question the current utility of those traditions. They know they will not win friends or collaborators if they show disrespect. Being respectful allows them to align with others in a way that provides opportunities to persuade or influence.
3. **Poise:** Professionals maintain poise when things get tough. They do not lose their cool over things that are frustrating or disappointing, even while they show passion for their position. This way, they earn admiration for their cool and gain credibility for their point-of-view, while avoiding turning off those who might be aggravated by unrestrained actions.
4. **Initiative:** Professionals are pro-active agents of change, not victims of circumstance. They take initiative to get things done. If they don't like how things are going, then they work

to change them. This may require forming a strategy to gain buy-in or seeking the blessings of people in authority. In the end, they simply do not let things wait that require attention.

5. **Discipline:** Professionals demonstrate discipline ---consistent application of purposeful effort --- in their behavior. They maintain pace on projects through careful allocation of their valuable time, energy and resources. They also maintain discipline to professional and organizational standards of conduct.
6. **Curiosity:** Professionals know that change is constant, and therefore they have a thirst for learning. They have to be humble enough to admit what they don't know. The curious manager shows both skepticism about what they are told, and imagination about what could be. Curiosity keeps them young. A learning mindset is a necessary and powerful force-multiplier for the professional who wants to do more than maintain the status quo.
7. **Compassion:** Professionals show compassion for others and themselves. No human is perfect; everyone makes mistakes. Compassion causes us to reach out and seek to help those who need a hand, and to forgive ourselves and others when mistakes are made. All that said, having compassion does not make the professional a doormat. Indeed, showing "tough love" and holding people accountable if they are falling on the job becomes more effective with compassion.
8. **Adaptability:** Professionals can adapt to the constantly changing conditions and nature of their work. They may be creative in their adaptability, or simply resourceful. Yet they do what they must to overcome obstacles whenever they find them rather than rigidly holding on to known ways and means.

Leadership Character Traits--Beyond Professionalism

Leadership requires more than Professional Character. Leaders must operate at a higher level. Their principles must be persistent to set the tone for the organization and support those that might not have representation.

9. **Passion:** Leaders have passion for their work. They are fully engaged, and role model full engagement. This serves to motivate others. At times when their own passion fades, they still find ways to force themselves to act with full-engagement, and this renews their own sense of passion.
10. **Objective:** Leaders work hard to seek truth, act fairly, and avoid bias and favoritism. They seek to understand the many obvious and not-so-obvious variables that affect others' behavior before passing judgment. They understand their own appropriate and inappropriate biases and seek to weigh them objectively so that their decisions and actions are fair.
11. **Resilience:** Leaders can bounce back from adversity. They can take a gut punch and get back into the game. They have had setbacks and have shown they can recover and endure. Resilience can only be learned from adversity. Show me a leader who has not been tested, and I'll show you one who does not know the extent of his/her own resilience.
12. **Courage:** Leaders have the courage to address issues of conflict and concern. They don't let their fears keep them from advancing the agenda. They can make tough decisions under pressure, even when others may want them to take the easy way out. While some leaders are required to demonstrate physical courage, the courage most required for business leaders is moral and intellectual courage: standing up, speaking up, and taking the highroad.

These Character Traits cannot simply reside in a manager as ideals. They must be actively lived and reinforced so that they become as easy to demonstrate as walking. This may take years of challenge and refinement.

Demonstrating these character traits on occasion is necessary for success; however, in order to achieve high-performance demonstrating these traits alone is not sufficient. Character must be *animated with Awareness* and *deployed with Versatility and Purposefulness* to best serve an organization and society.

The Character Clock

The Character Clock can be helpful for deploying your good character in real-life situations. Each of the 12 Key Character Attributes take the place of the hour markers. (See the image on the following page.) The **secondhand** sweeps around the clock face, passing each character attribute, reminding us to keep constant awareness of the desired leadership character. The **minute hand**, moving more slowly, reminds us that we should deploy our character attributes with flexibility or versatility, and not get stuck operating from one attribute only. The Hour hand, moving most slowly of all, places emphasis on slower evolution and purposefulness for how we both grow and use our character.

***Awareness* is the ability to observe and orient one's own actions and reactions as well as those of others**. Awareness provides the pivot-point that allows us to choose character traits and put them into service. Without awareness, character traits sit like an unopened encyclopedia of virtues: they are there, and there is no intelligence operating to indicate which book to open.

Awareness extends beyond immediate situations and can be considered as also operating on a continuum of time from ancient history through the present and generations into the future. Reflecting with awareness on the patterns of personal behavior in the context of history and society helps the individual to develop his/her character and to become more mature and refined in their ability to utilize the character traits to positive ends.

***Versatility* is the ability to choose which character trait most needs to be deployed, and how it will be used.** For instance, a loyal employee has been missing agreed-upon deadlines. This harms the team's effort. What character trait does the leader demonstrate: Discipline? Courage? Generosity? Loyalty? Compassion? Or perhaps some combination of the above? This is the value of having versatility. You will not be locked into only one way of addressing the situation.

***Purpose-full* is the ability to work towards sound goals that support a clear vision.** Leaders have a vision (their own, or one they have adopted from the wisdom of others). Leaders take on a mission to achieve this vision. They have a desire to make things better, to accomplish more, to persist in the face of adversity, and to push themselves and others to new heights in the service of what they view as the right mission. Purposefulness helps them to align their assets and mobilize proper methods to fulfill their vision.

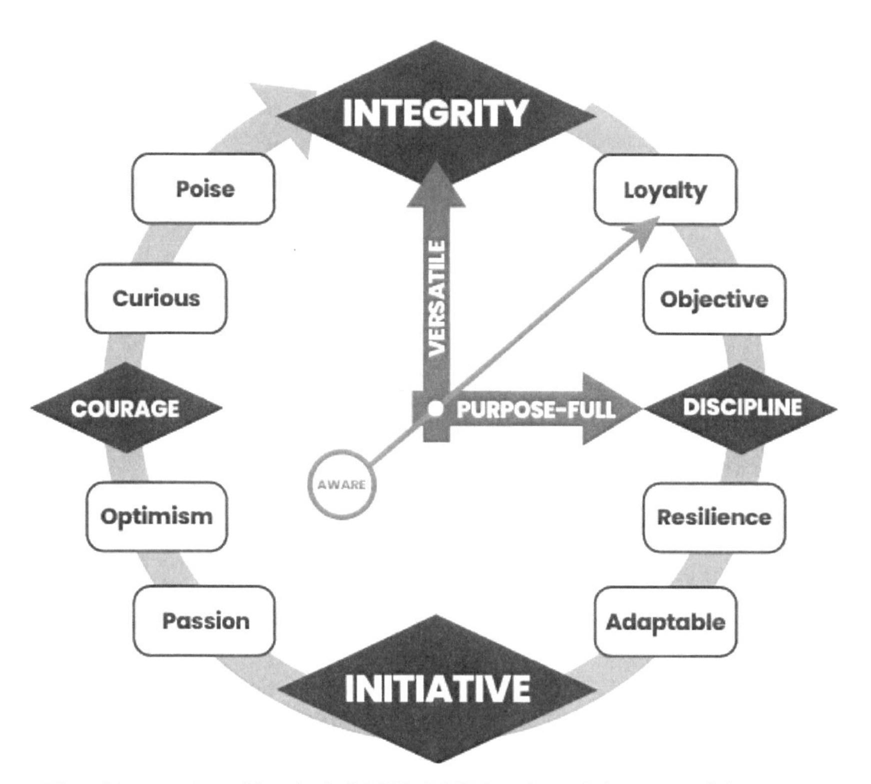

The Character Clock © 2007-2021 by Gerald A. Hutchinson Jr.

The best leaders possess the ability to maintain awareness of the situation and what character trait they need to use to get the best response from others.

BOOSTER CONCEPT

Post a list of character traits where you can refer to them. Mark up the ones that you particularly want to be conscious of, and purposeful about "owning." Try each day to find ways to act consistently with those character traits. Soon you will be doing so, and more importantly, you will be strengthening your character for the long haul.

THOUGHT STARTERS

- Describe for each of the character attributes one example of how you demonstrate that attribute.
- Now describe for each character attribute one way you can expand upon these attributes.

2

Deploying Your Strengths and Talents

Everyone has strengths and weaknesses, and we want to play from our strengths, and overcome or workaround our weaknesses. So, let's examine just what is a strength. The following simple exercise is a highly useful illustration of the concept of strengths.

- Take a piece of paper and sign your name as if on a document.
- Now sign your name with your eyes closed, just under the current signature.
- Now, switch the pen to your non-dominant hand and sign your name.
- Now look at the differences.

A strength can be done with almost no thought at all; it is practically automatic. In fact, it can be done with one's eyes closed!

A non-strength can still be performed, and it is awkward at best, and requires hard work and usually less competence. It requires a great deal of mental effort and focus [bandwidth], and the outcome is usually not nearly as accomplished.

Now, sign another person's name using your dominant hand and their own handwriting/signature style.

This is just a bit harder than signing your own name, and you can do it easily. This action illustrates a strength applied to a new situation.

The Power of Playing from Strengths

"Success is achieved by developing our strengths, not by eliminating our weaknesses."

Marilyn vos Savant

Imagine – just for a minute. What would happen if every significant person you interacted with at work --- you, your bosses (both previous and current), your leadership teams, your mentors, and your colleagues---were focused on all the things you were doing well at work? What would happen if they targeted your strengths, provided positive feedback on what you did well, and provided you with new opportunities, never saying or mentioning "weakness" to diminish who you are as a person?

How does this feel? What might a work environment, focused on strengths, look like? In a workplace like this, how would you respond to feedback that is both positive and constructive?

These are only some of the questions that come to mind when imagining a world that focuses on exploring your strengths, or said differently, your 'superpowers'.

Did you know that one of the key roadblock's companies are dealing with today is loss of talent due to bad managers? In fact, Gallup found that "70% of a team's engagement is influenced by managers." (Source: Ratanjee, V. 2021. *Why*

Managers Need Leadership Development Too. www.gallup.com/workplace/328460/why-managers-need-leadership-development.aspx)

Conventional wisdom holds that it can take five to seven positive work experiences to offset one negative experience in the workplace. This wisdom alone offers us so many different ways to understand true engagement in the workplace. Let's explore this optimistic approach that places value on strengths over weaknesses, and particularly how individual contributors, managers, leaders, and organizations can harness the value of leading with a person's strengths.

What would happen if your managers and leaders focused on what was RIGHT with you and not what was wrong with you in the workplace? This question kicked off Dr. Clifton's life-long journey exploring the concept of "Strengths." Dr. Clifton imagined this question after seeing dissatisfaction and disengagement in the workplace. He realized that sharing what's wrong with you is never as powerful or as motivating as sharing what's right with you. Henry Ford famously said: "Think you can or think you can't. Either way you will be proved right."

This discovery contributed to the creation of Gallup's ***CliftonStrengths®*** assessment. This assessment supports people by clarifying and then understanding their strengths at a deeper level. This guides individuals to explore how their strengths can support the way they lead, grow, and develop their talents.

To be clear, there are no simple solutions when solving for human behavior or talent management. However, what we've found in our careers and our coaching practices is that people like to add value and feel valued. You want to be valued and appreciated for your strengths. How will you demonstrate value and appreciation for the strengths of your peers, colleagues, direct reports, and your boss?

Many of the Saterman Connect coaches are certified Gallup ***CliftonStrengths®*** based coaches and leverage these methodologies in their coaching. The assessment illuminates your innate strengths, helps you understand the meaning of each strength, and identifies ways in which you can maximize these talents both personally and professionally.

Let's expand on this idea and use an analogy to provide some perspective. We often ask, "What's the strongest muscle in your body?" The answer usually is, "my brain, my heart, and even my jaw or tongue." All interesting answers, and in this case, it's not a trick question. What we are asking is, if you went to the gym and worked out the muscle that is the easiest to build in your body, what would that muscle be? Even after exercising a lot, you are not very sore. Perhaps it's your "quads".

The opposite might be your "biceps". Your biceps have never been your strongest muscle. If you had to move a piece of furniture, perhaps you would push it with your legs, not your arms. This is because you know innately that your lower body strength is stronger than your upper body strength.

Now, back to the concept of strengths and how best to utilize this new knowledge. Like your muscles, or in this case strengths, you can choose how to deploy them and understand their power as you grow, develop, and work them out throughout your life. We are focusing on "life," not work. These strengths are a part of you, always. You can't just choose when they will be part of you.

Gallup's ***CliftonStrengths®*** assessment specifies 34 strengths and there is a 1-in-33 million chance that someone else has the exact same Top 5 strengths that you have in the same order. It's just math. You are unique and your uniqueness does not fit into a box.

We are going to share an example of how the ***CliftonStrengths®*** model can be applied to your own development.

One of the 34 strengths is called "Activator". People with high Activator will create drive, bring motivation for getting started, need to move forward by doing, value initiative, and do not like wasting time. In other words, people with high Activator are quick to get started or spring into action. We might use the image of a car gas pedal to illustrate this strength.

Strengths are net neutral. This means being an Activator is neither positive nor negative. As a result, the questions you might ask included: How are your strengths or talent themes serving you? How are your strengths or talent themes holding you back?

Activator Example – Josh Saterman

> *Over the years, Josh received feedback that he could be intense, move too fast, provide ideas without asking for the data or sufficient background to decide. This is a perception others have of him versus the way he sees himself. This feedback is directly related to his Activator strength. Let's explore how.*
>
> *Remember, strengths by their very nature and definition are not positive or negative. When using a 'strength' to its best potential, we call this being on the mountain top. Think about it. When you are on*

the mountain top, you might want to sing, shout or celebrate your accomplishment. You also have a full vantage point of your surroundings. On the flip side, when a strength is being overused, misused, or misunderstood, you might be using a strength as an anchor. An anchor holds you in place, keeps you stuck in one position, and doesn't allow you to move forward.

When Josh received this feedback, he recognized he was using the Activator strength as an anchor. How could he re-frame the feedback to understand where he could re-deploy his superpower of "Activator" differently to become a stronger leader, manager, and teammate? Re-focusing, Josh approached the use of his Activator strength to create momentum, share an idea and rally colleagues around that idea. When bringing a strong sense of urgency, he pauses to explain why an idea or initiative is important and then shares the why, what, and how to drive an initiative forward. Remember the previous example of the gas pedal. A high Activator needs to always know how to set the pace. When do you slow down to allow others to follow, and when do you speed up to move forward and create a strong sense of urgency?

Josh loves initiative and instigation. In fact, he loves getting started more than he loves completing the actual work at times. He has learned over the years that he prefers to get things started and then pass them to the high "Achievers" who love to get stuff done. A power pair for him is someone with a high Achiever. We are a good team because, "I can get things started and they can help get things over

> *the finish line." (Side Note: Nettie is a high Achiever and that's one of the ways Saterman Connect gets initiatives both started and finished!)*
>
> *Once Josh re-framed this feedback, he was able to redirect the actions he owned and rethink how to approach scenarios, initiatives, and collaborative opportunities to raise his own anchor and push him back onto the mountain tops.*

Again, the intention of strengths is to provide a perspective and lens around you, your growth, and how you can prioritize your growth. They are intended to help you lead with your superpowers and not dwell on your "weaknesses". We have so many attributes and opportunities to lead with our best selves, and understanding our strengths allows us to do just that. Why not focus on your superpowers so that you can reach your own mountain top?

To learn more about Gallup's ***CliftonStrengths®*** reach out to us at: **SatermanConnect.com** and explore how we can support you and your team understanding and building your strengths.

BOOSTER CONCEPT
Find out your strengths! Use this information to play from your strengths rather than focusing on fixing your weaknesses.

THOUGHT STARTERS

- Compare and contrast a time when you were engaged versus disengaged at work? Share how this impacted your quality of work, felt value at work, and energy levels to support your colleagues?
- How can improving your team members' engagement improve your team's results?

- What are the strengths (or superpowers) you are most proud of and bring with you to work each day? How are you sharing and expressing these strengths with your colleagues to let them know what you do best?
- How are you and your team's strengths serving you? And how are these strengths holding you and your team back?

3

Building Your Individual Growth Plan

Doing the best at this moment puts you in the best place for the next moment.

Oprah Winfrey

A 90-day IGP gives you 12 weeks to work on your development with intentionality, and then a 13th week to evaluate progress and then reset for your next 90-days.

A growth plan is simple in the question it asks: ***Where do you want to intentionally focus your energies in the name of growth?***

The pandemic and technological change has proven that:

- The pace of change in the world is getting faster
- Exponential growth means technology will improve and that new technologies are only in their infancy stages
- Work and life are increasingly blending
- Change and uncertainty are ever present

Think about how many times you work from home. What about how many times you might need to take care of kids, elderly relatives, or loved ones? What about that early morning presentation with your boss, and your boss's boss? Life happens. Work happens.

Your growth plan must consider how you will embed your development opportunities into your life. You want to set realistic expectations and continue the evolution of your growth. This is how you build your toolbox then sharpen and refine the tools you need for your future. Therefore, your IGP needs to be flexible enough that it can morph or adapt to change. This gives time to reflect, redirect, and complete the next cycle of actions.

One mistake we've seen is trying to accomplish too much. It's a set-up for not achieving much when you think about the growth plan as this grandiose all-or-nothing document. By creating a growth plan that is too big or too broad, it becomes difficult to focus on smaller, specific, and manageable steps needed to create consistent, steady, and measurable progress.

Creating Your 90-Day IGP

A useful analogy comes from a tropical vacation of Parasailing, Snorkeling, and Scuba Diving. When parasailing you are getting the overview, maybe see where the fish are, where the ocean floor is deeper or shallower, where boats are located, and how they are from the shore.

When writing a growth plan, this is the time to think about the times you will be snorkeling and when you will scuba dive. Snorkeling is swimming on top of the water. Sure, you may dive for a few seconds here and there to get a closer look, and overall, you are distant enough to see a majority of what's in front of you. You are also close enough to make out the colors of fish, coral reef layout, the seabed, and the colors of the water close up.

Scuba diving is when you are closest. You don't see schools of fish, instead you see the individual fish you want to follow. Maybe you trail after a sea turtle or get a bit closer to that eel you find intriguing. You even run your hands through the sand on the ocean floor. I use this analogy because it helps you consider: Are you parasailing, snorkeling or scuba diving as you write your growth plan? What's the level of detail you wish to articulate? Remember who you are sharing this document with and how will they need to receive this information?

When writing your 90-Day IGP, begin with the end in mind. This is your snorkeling moment.

Step 1: The goal is to say what you've accomplished by day 90, so lay that out first. First identify three headline topics within a 90-day cycle. Anything more might be too much and anything smaller might not push you hard enough. This sets the tone for how to look at the other components necessary to get from day 1 to day 89. Slowly you are moving from skimming the waters and staking out the scenes in front of you. Then you move closer, you are making your way along the trail moving towards the goal or set of goals you established. Each month you'll want to connect what you are accomplishing in that month to move you to the next, and then the next, and finally to the end of month three.

Step 2: What type of job are you currently in? Why are you here? What will add value to an organization and why did they hire you? Transfer you? Promote you?

Oftentimes we look at this step as the 'consideration' step. There are typically four buckets that help to define what type of role you play within your organization. Are you a Change Agent, Pacesetter, Maintainer or Stabilizer?

- *A Change Agent* disrupts and moves a team and the organization in a different direction. This role is crucial for teams looking to make big changes or address a new opportunity with limited restrictions.
- *A Pacesetter* will set the tone. This is the person whose role it is to bring people along and sets the tempo for how fast (or slow) the team or organization moves forward. This is meeting people where they are at and helping them to see where they need to go.
- *A Maintainer* keeps things "steady as she goes". Keeping the status quo operating efficiently and not letting things get too far away from humming along nicely is hugely important for some operations. Some people are well-suited for this, while the type of person that needs novelty and excitement could likely botch this up.
- *A Stabilizer* is a leader that can put brakes on disorganization and chaos. This role is very important. Imagine if a part of the business model is broken, it might be your job to slow that bleeding and allow the organization to allocate their resources someplace else.

Considering what role you play within an organization or team is critical. And it may change over time. You may start off as a Stabilizer and find yourself down the road moving towards a Change Agent. You might be a Maintainer and then the world shifts, and you must become the Pacesetter. As a practice to consider - continue to monitor the pulse of your situation (also known as 'reading the room'), take stock with your colleagues or accountability partners to ensure your goals and consider your role within the team or the organization. Adapt your 90-Day IGP, as your situation changes.

To simplify and summarize — an Individual Growth Plan (90-Day IGP) answers the following questions:

1. What do I want to learn?
2. What does your manager, peers, or organization say you should be learning?
3. How will I build my growth plan to allow me to shine and grow?
4. What role do I play within the organization and how will my growth plan also complement the value-add I bring to an organization?

We accomplish more when we create bitesize goals and celebrate successes along the way. Giant leaps are nice, and the best learnings come from your journey. Metrics or benchmarks along the way are great ways to measure your success against your plan. You get to choose how you want to grow and develop your toolbox.

Some key points:

1. Growth is the priority, not accomplishing everything all at once. Strive to create goals that you can track or assign metrics.
2. Share your progress with your allies and influencers. They are your champions along the way.
3. Don't "boil the ocean," meaning don't try to do too much. Better to succeed at a few than fail at many. Commit to attainable goals that you control.
4. Celebrate the journey. Wins are worth remembering... Hint: they are also the best practices to study.

5. Take the time to reflect on what made you successful. How will you duplicate your own best practices? How will you share these best practices with your team, peers, and colleagues?
6. Ensure you purposefully create time to share your 90-Day IGP with your direct supervisor. Bring them along on this journey. This builds buy-in and supports accomplishing your goals.

Using this format establishes a realistic timeline to measure success. Within those 12-13 weeks you are capable of building intentional moments individually, and with key stakeholders, to track your progress and embed your newfound development into your way of being.

These instructions will provide guidance on how to create your 90-Day IGP.

Consider the goals that are most important for you to develop. Perhaps ask your accountability partners to share feedback with you on the key areas they would like to see you develop. This 90-day IGP (or any growth plan for that matter) should use the SMART(ER) goals — Specific. Measurable. Achievable. Relevant. Time-based. *Follow up with*: (Evaluate. & Reset.)

The 90-Day IGP is set up into sections:

1. **Strengths:** List out your hallmark strengths or dominant talent themes. This can remind you of how you execute, think, influence, and build relationships. If you haven't completed your Gallup ***CliftonStrengths®*** assessment, contact us at **SatermanConnect.com** to work 1:1 with a certified coach.
2. **Topics** (or Goals): These 1-2-3 topics are limited to three because you want to sign yourself up for bite-size goals.

3. **Plans:** Plans define the set of actions that will allow you to accomplish your goals. These plans are the ways you want to act or think differently. If you do X, Y, and Z, then you will accomplish 1, 2, and 3.
4. **Actions:** Actions are the impacts you wish to accomplish. They are measurable, time-based, and allow you to look back and measure your success.

   NOTE: The Plan is your intention. The Action is your impact.

These four sections of the growth plan are focused and limited to one page. This is to keep you aware that not everything can be solved within 90 days. This tool can support you in separating what's "nice-to-have" from what's needed. Some topics, plans, and actions might need to be placed into a parking lot for a later date.

To explore different templates and models to support your 90-Day IGP, visit **SatermanConnect.com** to download a version that works for you.

BOOSTER CONCEPT
Taking the time to construct an IGP has a tremendous impact for you down the road. It is like compound interest. Every bit of development you can do earlier in your career leverages into greater impact later on. It is a great example of "Going Slow to Go Fast" -- Put your time in now, and go fast later!

THOUGHT STARTERS

- How do you like to create bite-sized goals?
- What are you learning about yourself through creating your 90-Day IGP?

- What best practices are you learning to implement for yourself? How are these best practices and disciplines demonstrating strong leadership for your team to emulate?
- What are the benefits to sharing your 90-Day IGP with your peers, accountability partners, and your direct supervisor?

4 Mapping Your Social Matrix

Success isn't about how much money you make;
it's about the difference you make in people's lives.

Michelle Obama

Your behavior and success are impacted by those with whom you surround yourself. Some people are essential for your success, others less so. This is not about who you like; rather, this is about who will support you and get you to accomplish your goals and the company's goals. Understanding who you are hanging out with, and how much, can give you useful insight into new ways to prioritize your use of time. The below chart will support you in objectively laying out your social sphere. It will also help you consider who your accountability partners are so you can lean on them to support your own growth.

Fundamentally, in the work world, there are four general categories of persons that can impact your success: (1) those who are *Mission Critical* for your success, (2) those *Important* for your success, (3) those who may *Possibly Impact* your success, and (4) those who are *Not Connected* to your success.

We can describe the degree of connection that you can have with those people (1) on your *"Dream Team"*, (2) *Close*

Contacts, (3) *General Associates*, and (4) *Others*. Use a version of the following table and populate it with persons who are in your social sphere. This way, you can determine who you may want to make closer contact with, and who you may need to step back from spending as much time with.

How to know and distinguish between the Levels of Connections:

- Mission Critical - These are the ones that you must have great connection to in order to get the job done as smoothly as possible, as quickly as possible.
- Important - Their influence is often task-limited, or of special expertise. They may be gatekeepers that you need to have on your side enough to get through the red tape.
- Possible Impact - Persons who may hold some special influence, and you are unsure how much.
- Not Connected - People that do not seem to have any direct impact on your work.

How to know and distinguish the Degree of Connection:

- Dream Team - Your "critical few" that you feel that you absolutely have on your team. Generally, not more than 7 people.
- Close Contacts - Persons that you know well enough to have a decent grasp of who they are and what they can do
- General Associates - Persons that you may have a bit of familiarity with, or that some of your Dream Team can vouch for.
- Others - Basically, anyone else...some may be distractions, others may move all the way to Dream Team.

YOUR SOCIAL MATRIX	**Mission Critical**	**Important**	**Possible Impact**	**Not Connected**
Dream Team				
Close Contacts				
General Associates				
Others				

NOTE: Even if someone is "Not Connected" to you for your work success, they may be essential for your mental and social health.

Many people have friends that simply do not have a direct impact at all on their work life and are part of their 'essential inner circle' for friendship, camaraderie, and just blowing off steam where the stakes have zero impact on work success. In other words, they are treasures on another island. Also, just because you do not recognize the current immediate value of an individual does not mean that tomorrow, they may turn out to be hugely important for your success. An axiom about organizational life that is useful to remember: Be kind to all on your way up, because you are likely to see them again. Don't burn bridges.

BOOSTER CONCEPT #1
Mapping out where you think you stand with folks can clearly reveal gaps. The folks around you are your team for success. Without knowledge of who your strong players are and who you are spending time with, you will continue with your own unconscious pattern.

BOOSTER CONCEPT #2
Don't be a suck-up.

THOUGHT STARTERS

- How do you know who is mission critical to you getting your job done?
- In what ways will this social sphere update and shift over time?

5
Preparing for Your Team

Give me six hours to chop down a tree and I will spend the first four sharpening the axe.

Abraham Lincoln

The most important variable in the strength of a team is the quality of leadership. As we have already discussed, make sure that you understand and can fully deploy your leadership platform. To get the most out of your people, seek to understand them. Come to know their strengths and their weaknesses. Watch them, listen to them, and feel where they are coming from emotionally and how they can impact others.

Make sure that you maintain humility about your own position as the leader of your team. You are replaceable, and you are dispensable. And if you adopt a better-than-thou attitude, then you likely will not get the performance from them that you desire. This does not mean that you have to give up your role as leader in order to be "equal" to your team. It does mean that you must have perspective about how much you can in fact be their leader. You may be assigned the position as a leader, and you must earn their respect.

Soft Skills are Critical Skills

The US military invented the term "soft skills" to describe and separate them from the "hard skills" of climbing ladders, operating machinery, and other tasks that required physical labor. We are passionate about calling 'Soft Skills', 'Critical Skills'. Here's why:

> In the world of organization development and leadership coaching, "soft skills" are a combination of people skills, social skills, communication skills, character or personality traits, attitudes, mindsets, career attributes – fundamentally social and emotional intelligence capabilities that enable people to navigate their environment, work well with others, perform well, and achieve their goals with complementing hard skills. "Soft skills" are human skills. Connecting, engaging, influencing, and gaining the hearts, minds, and motivated actions of others.

Here's the deal. These soft skills are **NOT** soft. **They are critical.** You are required to deal with people, have common sense, possess a positive attitude, listen with intention, act appropriately, be inclusive, act with respect, and more. These skills, competencies even, are critical to getting your job done.

Leaders, true leaders, do not think of these skills as nice. They are **necessary** because critical skills are all about connecting, supporting, and developing partners, peers, and employees. **In today's environment, you simply cannot drive effectively nor thrive as a leader without critical skills.**

> ***Let's share an example: Listening.*** *Listening is not a soft skill. Rather, this is a critical skill to being an effective leader, collaborator, peer, and human.*

> *Listening connects us and allows us to see other perspectives to make more informed and educated decisions. Listening allows others to feel heard, valued, and part of the team. Listening is not soft. Listening is critical.*

Section 2

DRIVE.

Delivering Results with Your Team

1
Driving as a Leader

What is success? I think it is a mixture of having a flair for the thing that you are doing; knowing that it is not enough, that you have got to have hard work and a certain sense of purpose.

Margaret Thatcher

Having heightened awareness of your Platform is powerful. You understand your situation and build your team. Now let's turn to Driving for Results through action.

But just to reiterate the point, it's important that your team knows and understands your Platform. Transparency about your Platform builds trust because they will see you leading the way with vulnerability. For those uneasy about opening to others, just know that you don't have to share everything about yourself, all your secrets and peccadillos. But at least opening up about your "why," your skill set, and your values will go a long way to inspiring them to authentically get on board and follow you.

Look at this from the opposite perspective: who would want to follow a leader that they know nothing about?! That level of willful blindness is the mark of a person with no stakes in the game, little engagement, basically someone like a robot who will blindly follow whatever they have been programmed to do.

And that person lacks the initiative and engagement to really help you drive to get the results you will need to continue to grow your career.

Many emerging managers are tempted to follow the mantra: *"If you want something done right, then do it yourself."* This mindset will lead to your failure. You can only achieve what you need to achieve with a team, and that means relying on the team. And a team, just like a garden, needs tending to make sure it has the right growth conditions to get a great fruitful harvest.

In other words, DRIVE is about guiding, supporting, and growing your team. As a leader, you have an obligation to set up the conditions so they can perform at their best to be productive in the areas of necessary importance to achieve organizational goals. If they are not being productive, you have to look no further than in the mirror to find the cause.

So, what are the conditions to set up your team for success? Here are the essentials.

2
Building Your Team

Great things in business are never done by one person. They're done by a team of people.

Steve Jobs

As a manager you cannot succeed alone - you must have a team. It will take the unified work of a 'team' to accomplish your goals in corporate America. Therefore, make sure that your team is as great as it can be. But before we get into the key steps of building and developing your team, let's focus on you, the leader.

***Leadership* is the primary factor in team success.**

Earning your team members' trust and respect increases your influence. Remember, the simplest definition of leadership is influence. So, to influence them more, you cannot rely on your position-power/authority, or even your expertise alone. They must also trust and respect you, holding you in positive regard as their manager and as a person of character; they need to have trust that you will be doing the right thing for them, and working for the team as a whole.

Keep in mind what is known as the Pygmalion effect. This states that people will live up to or down to the expectations that others have of them. Therefore, as a leader if you set small stretch expectations for them, they will be more likely to live up to them. You will need to use judgment in determining how much of a stretch that they can handle without breaking them.

As a leader, understand that structure creates behavior. This bears repeating: structure creates behavior. What this means is that how you structure your team's workday, work week, and work month will have a huge impact on what they are able to accomplish. The leader who is smart and savvy about structuring activity is one who builds habits of success and best practices that can sustain success.

BOOSTER CONCEPT
Work to grow yourself as a leader. Read books, listen to podcasts, work with a coach. Leadership development is a lifetime process. The sooner you consciously work at becoming a better leader, the sooner you will be a better leader.

Truths about Teams

Culture Beats Strategy

You may have a brilliant strategy. A real game-changer. But if your team is unable or unwilling to deliver on that strategy, then your brilliance simply cannot be accomplished. You may have heard the expression that culture eats strategy for breakfast, lunch, and dinner. Fundamentally, this means that the stronger and more agile your team, the more that they will be self-directing and accomplishing strategic objectives independent of a formal strategy. In other words, they automatically adapt to the situation and adopt the best strategy to achieve their goals.

A savvy manager would rather spend more time developing their people, and the culture of the team, than thinking through and thinking up a fantastic strategy. Note: Culture *accelerates* strategy because the team seeks out and thinks through the current constraints, challenges, and opportunities and forecasts probable success-strategies for the future, then acts on them.

How do you develop and reinforce culture?

> *Define the culture* that you really want to create on your team. Make sure it is fully aligned with that of the organization. Consider the points of culture that need special attention to achieve your team goals. And understand that a team of average players that is fully unified around a central achievable goal and can communicate effectively is far superior in its performance than a team of rock stars who are not unified and who not do not communicate well.
>
> *Structure and attain culture-promoting behaviors.* These are the behaviors that are required to achieve the culture that you want. This means looking specifically at how each team member spends their time each day. If you see inconsistencies in skills, competencies, and behaviors of a high performing culture, then do what you must do to structure behaviors and build skills to achieve that high performance.
>
> *Reward culture-promoting behaviors* that are completely consistent with the culture that you want to create. What are useful rewards? What does recognition look like? Simple recognition of good work is a powerful motivator. Some people prefer to be recognized and rewarded directly by their leader. Others prefer public recognition. Giving praise, high fives, smiling, and written statements of appreciation are powerful motivators and

reinforcements for the types of behavior that you want to cultivate. More complex rewards and recognition can include company awards voted on by fellow team members, special activities such as a team picnic, a night on the town, or other fun celebrations.

Finally, realize that people respond to incentives, such as recognition. Reinforce that which you wish to have repeated.

BOOSTER CONCEPT
Great culture starts with selecting great people. If your people already possess the attributes and values that create great culture, then it is a lot less work to just create those structures that will reinforce the good things and suppress the bad parts of human nature. Always be on the lookout for bad behavior and nip it in the bud. It is toxic to a great culture.

Inclusion, Equity, and Belonging are Essential for Promoting Diversity and Unity

It's no secret that inclusive and united teams outperform their peers in team-based assessments. There are books, articles, podcasts, and more dedicated to demonstrating how inclusive teams have stronger sales growth, increased profitability, more cash flow per employee, higher retention, and more. Diversity, equity, inclusion, and belonging (D.E.I.B.) requires leading with integrity, initiative, unity, and we know it drives stronger business results. Leading with a D.E.I.B. lens also creates a strong, sustainable, high-performance culture. Let's define these terms for enhanced clarity and understanding.

Diversity (D) is a fact. If you have two humans in the same room, you have a diverse room. Diversity is also defined by looking at what's visible as well as invisible about a person. We refer to this as the dimensions of your diversity. Think of it like peeling an onion. You see what's on the outside and as you go deeper into the onion you see the layers. Some people will also refer to this as an iceberg. You see the tip of the iceberg; however, the most significant part of the iceberg is what's floating below the surface of the waterline.

Equity (E) is a value that centers on the quality of being fair and objective. This is not equality. Equality is sameness. Equity is fairness.

Inclusion (I) is a choice. This is a behavior where you provide, through your policies, equal access, resources, and opportunities to any person who might otherwise be or feel excluded or marginalized.

Belonging (B) is a feeling. You create that feeling over time and consistent behavior. This is an emotion, and it comes from being comfortable expressing ideas, sharing experiences, creating psychological safety, and contributing, knowing your input is valued. Belonging is not an end goal — belonging is an ever-present journey that can always be nurtured.

These four words, Diversity, Equity, Inclusion, and Belonging, are often used like a 'to-do' list. Think of this as an evolving cultural journey versus a singular destination. Like life, as you grow, learn, and develop so does your understanding of how, as a leader, you will influence and impact D.E.I.B.

Start moving forward by learning with an open mind and heart, asking questions, not being afraid to be vulnerable, sharing stories, and educating yourself.

We've created four buckets to complement this journey:

- Building Awareness
- Creating Connection
- Embracing Diversity
- Opening Minds

Each of these four buckets are ways to think about your organization and how you are embedding D.E.I.B. into the way you behave, think, act, and grow.

This chart, developed by SatermanConnect, demonstrates how like an "onion" the lens of D.E.I.B. impacts our workforce, workplace, and marketplace.

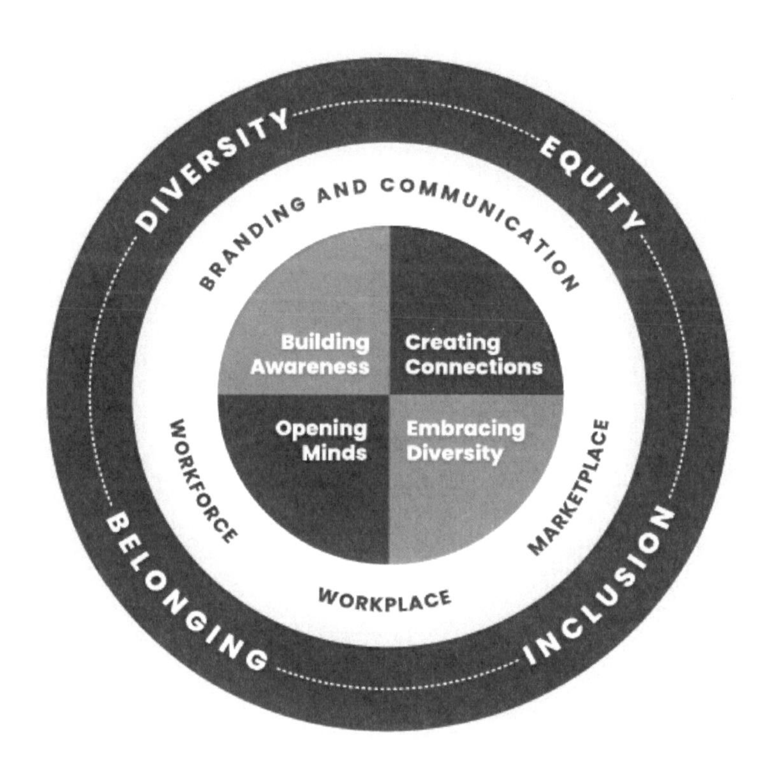

Building Awareness: There's no substitute for talking to each other to build awareness and truly open our hearts and minds. We learn about each other through the stories that we share, and it is easier said than done.

OPTIONS/EXAMPLES: Workshops, Panel Discussions, D&I Forums, Micro-learning, Metrics and Benchmarks

Creating Connections: To thrive and succeed long -term you need to create robust connections between your people and your organization's values at every level.

OPTIONS/EXAMPLES: BeyondBoardingTM , Talent Acquisition, Onboarding, Leadership and Professional Development

Embracing Diversity: This is all about acknowledging that people are different, and our differences are good. Innovation, creativity, awareness, and awakening create the business success stories of tomorrow. By embracing diversity, you can champion new possibilities and new growth for your employees and your organization.

OPTIONS/EXAMPLES: Diversity Council, Cultural Fluency, Global History and Heritage, Customer Experiences

Opening Minds: Many of us bring unconscious bias and other pre-existing models with us to the workplace. But none of us can know what we don't know.

OPTIONS/EXAMPLES: B+ERGs, Recognition, Coaching and Feedback Models, Performance Management

Sometimes, team members wonder if they really are part of a team. Perhaps they are new and have not acclimated yet. Or they may be working remotely and feel a sense of working alone. How do they see themselves? Why do they feel or not feel part of the team? Are they insiders, or are they outsiders? As a leader you have an obligation to make sure that all team members feel a sense of belonging and are part of the team.

What makes individuals become members of the team? It is up to you and the team to establish that criteria. When we think about inclusion, we often think about attributes which may be completely tangential to the functioning of a team. Open-mindedness for allowing individuals to state their opinions should be encouraged, as this diversity helps people see things from different perspectives. Some individuals may not feel comfortable with others' opinions about what the team is striving to do, or how it should go about doing those things. And there are people who simply do not want to contribute or engage, or who do not quite possess the social skills that will allow them to be an effective team member. When situations like this happen, you may need to figure out how to solve the problem, and if necessary, involve HR. You never know the underlying factors that cause these situations.

Later, we will talk about how to construct a *Team Charter* that identifies a variety of different elements that help the team to operate fairly and consistently.

BOOSTER CONCEPT

Crafting the Team Charter involves everyone and allows the team to know what is expected from each of them to help everyone on the team feel included and successful. Realize that everyone can struggle in some areas (though it may not be regarding actual team activity), and that compassion and respect are warranted for all.

> **Shameless Self-Promotion**: Saterman Connect can support you in creating connections through every part of the employee lifecycle. We offer a range of programs, workshops, and tools to support leaders and organizations by embedding D.E.I.B. initiatives into all competencies, policies, and initiatives within an organization. The programs, workshops, and tools help your employees see the world and the issues being discussed through a fresh, open lens. This is all about unlocking the power of your people to unlock business results.

Communication – The Powerhouse Nutrient of Teamwork

Communication nourishes teamwork. Without strong, effective, timely, accurate, and useful information, teams simply cannot operate at a high level of performance and productivity. Team members need constant communication to nourish both relationships and the ability to be productive. Communication has both formal structured elements, as well as informal and unstructured opportunities. In the absence of opportunities for informal and unstructured communication to occur, the need for structured communication opportunities becomes even more important.

A consistent cadence of team meetings is a necessity. The appropriate frequency comes in part from the urgency of the work: communication may be needed hourly, twice daily, or daily. The team meeting may last anywhere from ten minutes to an hour depending upon the situation and the demands for team performance. These may occur in the form of "Stand Up" meetings just to check in, huddle, touch base, and clarify what is going on that the team must respond to. These informal team meetings should not take the place of necessary communications between any other two team members to perform their jobs well. It will be up to the leader of the team to assure that these types of team meetings happen.

BOOSTER CONCEPT

Do Not -- repeat -- DO NOT rely on the concept that a meeting must take place in a meeting room, that it must be structured in 1-hour increments, or that it must occur specifically at the beginning or the end of the day or the week. Stand-Up meetings are fine. Video and teleconferencing are fine. Find the best time and way that suits the demands of the team so that the weekly team meeting and the daily team huddles can be effective for your unique situation.

Consistency Generates Confidence

As a leader it is essential that you maintain consistency in your activities so long as those are clearly oriented to high performance and success. Constant variation in routines means that some portion of mental bandwidth is no longer dedicated to solving the problems; instead, mental energy must be directed to merely adapting to varying methods, processes, practices and routines. It is also true that constant change is disruptive to mastering the nuance required to achieve mastery and high-performance teamwork.

BOOSTER CONCEPT

Be consistent with structures such as team huddles, and weekly meetings so that everyone knows what is going on. Be consistent in reviewing the Team Charter and holding the team to behaviors that assure team success. Be consistent in your insistence that the team work to the stated deliverables. But be willing to adapt to differing methods if, and only if, a compelling case can be made that it will get better results.

Critical Knowledge: Who is in the Driver's Seat?

To provide continuity of action, it's important to have an established order of who's in the Driver's seat. Although this may sound rigid and authoritarian, it's quite practical and doesn't require great formality — something as simple as designating someone who will make urgent decisions in the absence of the team leader.

BOOSTER CONCEPT

Make sure the team fully understands the ownership of authority when you are not directly at the helm. This reduces confusion about "who's in charge." Also, make sure that the limits of that authority are understood so that the person at the helm doesn't overstep their authority and make a stupid decision.

The More Team Members Own, They Better They Perform

Team members should have shared accountability. They need to have a sense of ownership in the outcomes. The more clearly you can establish who owns what when it comes to deliverables, the clearer it will be how to lead and manage them. Some people will operate better completely independently of others. Some will do better by having a work-buddy that they must collaborate with to achieve a deliverable. Whatever you do, the leader must clarify and gain commitment in the form of ownership for achieving the deliverables.

BOOSTER CONCEPT

Establish individual meetings with each team member to think through what the team can achieve. Get their input. Listen carefully. Help them take ownership of the team's performance by asking how they will assure success. The

more they shoulder the process, the less you have to lead directly.

What To Do When You Inherit an Existing Team

In case you do not get the chance to select your own team members, the following points may help you improve the team's performance:

Listen & Learn. Ask plenty of questions about what has worked and should be continued, what things need to be started to achieve higher performance, and what things perhaps should be stopped because they get in the way or hinder higher performance. Conduct a SWOT analysis (Strengths, Weaknesses, Threats, Opportunities) about the department, function, or unit that you are inheriting. The more questions you ask, the more information you will possess. Therefore, you will be empowered to make better decisions to support overall team productivity, as well as understanding the strengths and gaps impacting each team member.

A New Leader Assimilation process is great for both new or recently promoted leaders to help them smoothly transition into their new role and team. The goal of this process is to:

1. 'Jumpstart' these critical relationships and ensure the new leader is on the right track from the very beginning.
2. Create a climate of trust, openness, and honesty for the leader and the team.
3. Address questions, concerns or issues the team may have and the new leader needs to address.

The ultimate outcome of this process is to promptly encourage and facilitate two-way communication between the team and their new leader.

During this one-day session, facilitated by HR or an outside consultant, both the team and the leader have very specific roles. The Team's Role is to:

- Ask the tough questions
- Provide insight into the critical issues facing the team and the site
- Deliver actionable feedback to allow the new leader to understand how he/she is being perceived

The New Leader's Role is to:

- Share information on his/her leadership style, expectations, and goals for the team
- Answer questions and respond to feedback
- Clarify and discuss issues that emerge

NOTE: For details on how the process works, use this *Jumpstart New Leader and Team Effectiveness through the NLA Process* (Major, R., 2017. LinkedIn, retrieved from https://www.linkedin.com/pulse/jumpstart-new-leader-team-effectiveness-through-nla-robert/)

<u>Reinforce Culture</u>. Review how well the team is executing the behaviors that are consistent with a high performing culture. Find out if there are gaps and if so, how much needs to be changed to bolster behaviors and fill those gaps. Remember a high performing culture is far superior to a brilliant strategy, because the team members themselves will figure out what they must do to fulfill the strategy.

Use your Onboarding Period to Experiment. When you come into an existing team, you will have a honeymoon period that may last from 0-90 days. Your hiring manager should share what sort of Onboarding period you are likely to receive. This time period will impact your leadership approach. Use this period carefully and with intention to create trust, integrity, and credibility. One of the worst things a leader can do is behave with arrogance and dictatorial tones that create a "There's a new Sheriff in town!" mentality.

Leverage your Onboarding period as an opportunity to experiment with new ways of doing things and building buy-in within the team. First, understand the legacy approaches the team used to navigate its workdays, work weeks, and work months. Then, ask questions and understand where the team has gaps. And finally, set the expectations you will be experimenting with new ways, and that team members are expected to provide time and feedback to work things through together.

Key Partner Meetings are a process initiated by the new hire's manager that provides targeted conversations to support the new hires' assimilation into the organization. The goal of the meetings (within the first 30 days) is to help the new hire be more effective on-the-job and within the organization by providing advice, feedback, and information. These meetings will provide insight and support the new hire's assimilation into the organization, both formally and informally.

- Focus on Strengths. As you get to know your team members, focus on their strengths. Another chapter in this book talks about the power of strengths. Remember, when people are working from their strengths, they do a much better job and the work should be easier for them to accomplish. Look around and establish your expectations, consider "In what ways can I get my team members to engage in their work from positions of strength?" rather than trying to bolster a weakness.

- Devise Workarounds for Challenges. We prefer the term challenges over weaknesses because there are always ways to turn challenges into opportunities and learn how to lead from your strengths. Should you find weaknesses on the team, it is important to leverage the talents and strengths in others to close those gaps. The data on operating from strengths has revealed that it is simply much more powerful to get people to work from their strengths, rather than learn how to handle their weaknesses. You may not be able to find workarounds for a potential weak area in your team, and therefore figuring out how to redeploy your team members' effort may be required. Remember there are differences in gaps and weaknesses. An employee might require a new talent or a moment to learn in support of them closing this gap.

An example to support this concept.

> *Imagine a lawyer on your team working at the firm. This person is critically proficient in the law. However, this person might have a gap in their understanding of Intellectual Property, or IP law. If this person doesn't understand IP law, and IP law was required to do their job, that might be considered a weakness. However, because we know this person demonstrates critical acumen as an attorney, consider an approach focusing on education and training. (Examples: extend additional education through attending conferences, partnering with someone in the firm*

> *with IP experience). These are ways to support this person closing their gap.*
>
> *The idea here is to separate how you as a leader can support an employee with gaps versus simply looking at gaps through the lens of weakness that cannot be corrected.*

Building a High-Performing Team

The Framework

To build anything you need a framework. For a team, six key components form the framework that will ensure you are putting all the right pieces in place from the start.

We have all been on good teams and bad teams. On a "good" or "great" team everything runs smoothly. The team is connected, understands its mission, vision, values, and goals. They trust each other and take a collaborative approach to get things done to be successful. They are a well-oiled machine.

On a "bad" or "ineffective" team everyone could tell you what has gone wrong. Why are they disconnected, non-collaborative, or lack trust? There are many reasons that can cause a team to be ineffective, dysfunctional, or not behaving as a team at all.

Where do you start? In the beginning --- by understanding what it takes to build a high-performing team, from the ground up.

So, you are thinking, "Please tell me what the framework is for creating an effective team." Before we begin identifying the components of this framework, let's get alignment with the definition of "team."

A Team is a group of people that works together to achieve a common goal.

This definition does not say anything about being collaborative, trusting, responsive, or goal-oriented, and as managers and leaders this is what we strive for, and more. Here is where the framework comes into play. Let's identify the various components of the framework and then walk through the ways in which you will use these components to build a high-performing team.

Building Your Team Charter

The Team Charter sets out why the team was formed, the problem it is trying to solve, and how this problem fits in with the broader objectives of the organization. This serves as the compass for your team and contains the following information -- explained below.

The precise format of team charters varies from situation to situation and from team to team. And while the final charter document can take on many forms, much of the value of the Charter comes from thinking through and agreeing on the various elements.

Adapt the following elements based on your team's situational context.

- Context
- Mission and Vision
- Team Objectives
- Values
- Composition and Roles
- Resources and Support
- Operations
- Authority and Boundaries
- Negotiation and Agreement

Let's look at each of these elements in more detail.

Context

The Context is the introduction to the charter - Why the team was formed, the problem it's trying to solve, how this problem fits in with the broader objectives of the organization, and the consequences of the problem going unchecked. It answers the following questions: What problem is being addressed? What results or deliverables are expected? Why is this important? How will we achieve alignment?

Next, the Charter specifies:

- **Mission, Vision**: Identifies what the team wants to achieve long-term and how to get there
- **Team Objectives**: Identifies how the team will achieve its mission and the major milestones it desires to reach
- **Values**: Identifies the beliefs/principles of the team and can be used to hold people accountable to the team
- **Benefits:** What the overall benefits to the organization will be as a result of this group.
- **Measure of Success:** Identifies the qualitative and quantitative ways that success will be determined

- **Composition and Roles:** Defines the skills and desired experience of team members -- NOTE: the mission and Objectives helps determine who is needed on the team to accomplish the goals; specific roles and responsibilities
- **Authority and Boundaries:** Identifies what the team members can and cannot do to achieve the goals; time allocation, conflict resolution, recruiting, and approval processes
- **Resources and Support:** Resources available to the team to accomplish its goals. This includes budgets, time, equipment, and people
- **Operations**: How the team will operate on a day-to-day basis; what are the critical next steps to consider and who will own each of the defined roles and deliverables
- **Communication:** How the team will communicate, both with each other and how often; when will you involve key partners, other resources, and audiences — how will you and your team lead by influencing through strong communication

NOTE: You can expect there will be ongoing discussion and negotiation from team members, sponsors, and key partners throughout the process of creating the Charter. The goal is alignment. Once all are satisfactorily in alignment, the Charter is signed and enacted.

Creating Core Metrics

Metrics drive your team to meet the goals, key indicators, or other measurements set by the organization, your function, and the department. For example, what is your vision for your team at the end of this year? What metrics do you need in place to ensure you accomplish this vision and can be used to measure your success?

When creating your metrics use the SMARTER organizing theme to ensure you are not reaching too high or unable to meet the timeframe.

Specific: Who, What, Where, When, Why, Which

- Define the objective as much as possible with no ambiguous language. It should be an observable action or clear achievement. Action verbs help to describe the performance expected.

Measurable: From and To

- Can you track and measure outcomes? Describes what completion of that objective would look like (a rate, number, percentage, frequency, etc.).

Achievable: The Goal is in Reach for the Team

- Is the objective reasonable enough to be accomplished? How so? Make sure the goal is not out of reach and seen as unattainable without compromising safety or ethics.

Relevant: Worthwhile to Accomplish the Mission

- Is the objective consistent with other goals you have established and fits with your immediate and long-term plans? Evaluate objectives to ensure they are aligned with the company's priorities and organizational cascades.

Time-Bound: When / Deadline

- Your objective should include a time limit (start and completion). It will establish a sense of urgency and prompt you to have better time management.

Evaluate: Assess the Goal and What was Accomplished

- Your evaluation is a way to determine how to approach your next growth plan or learning opportunity.

Reset: Begin Again

- The growth and learning journey never ends. It's not that the bar keeps getting higher, rather think of it as building a stronger foundation to your pyramid or structure. With each brick laid, or leadership skill set enhanced, you are rising higher and higher in your growth. Why not think about what's next in your path to greater success.

Recognizing Key Skills and Competencies

Your team is the most critical tool you have to achieve success in that vision. Some key questions to ask yourself:

- Who are your high potentials?
- Who are your mediocre players?
- What are the different skill sets and competencies of each?
- What are the most important skills/competencies you'll need on your team for extraordinary success in meeting your vision, and the goals along the way?

If you can answer these questions and clarify the most important skills and competencies you need to achieve success, then you have begun to build this third component of your framework. Remember, these will be leadership, job, and technical skills and competencies.

Once the skills and competencies for each of the roles are identified the next thing to focus on, as you continue to build your team, is career mapping for each position.

Career Mapping is not an easy task. It is something that takes time, thought, and vision.

- What is the next level to achieve once an employee has mastered the skills and competencies of the job? Are these positions existing or do they need to be built out?
- Do I have well-written job descriptions with specifics?
- What are the required skills and competencies?
- What level of competency does this position require for each of the skills identified?
- What types of learning and development are needed to build the requisite skills and competencies?

These are just a few of the things to ask yourself as you are identifying and building out the core skills and competencies for each of the roles with the intention of creating career maps for each job.

Exploring Disparities on Your Team

This step is about conducting a "gap analysis." Getting clear on the gaps or disparities on your team that may hinder it to some degree in building a well-rounded and structured organization. With gaps come weaknesses. These weaknesses may take the form of missing key skills and competencies, building strengths where you do not have them, or perhaps bringing in outside expertise that is missing from the team. A gap analysis reinforces the importance of exploring the disparities of your team.

There are a number of assessments, such as Gallup's *CliftonStrengths*®, or the *Predictive Index*®, that are available to help you better understand your individual team members' strengths and provide an overall picture of the skills and competencies your team may be missing. Of course, you can do this on your own. However, these types of assessments can take it further, and make it easier for you. They will also help you to identify how best to communicate with individual team members, how individuals process or receive information, all critical components in managing and developing your team members, and creating cohesiveness, collaboration, and trust among the team.

Gaps typically arise when managers hire "people like themselves" instead of identifying the different personalities, skills, strengths and expertise the team requires to function at its fullest.

Below are a few questions to help you get started:

- What do I wish I had on my team that I don't have?
- Where is the team in terms of analytical skills?
- Who are our relationship builders? Mentors? Peer coaches?
- Who thinks strategically and provides the team direction?
- Who are our doer's versus thinkers?
- Who are our future managers when I look at succession planning for the team?

Consider answering these questions to begin your gap analysis.

Talent Acquisition

You know what the structure of your team needs to look like now and into the future. You have mapped out the roles and created career maps. And you recognize the skill and competency disparities on the team. Now it is time to make sure you have the budget to hire the 'right' people – and that your salary range is comparable to your competitors and other similar jobs.

This step requires a strong partnership with your talent acquisition team. It all begins with knowing what you are looking for, detailed with a great job description. Here are a few tips and tricks for creating engaging, culture-focused, and unbiased job descriptions:

1. Start with what you want the individual to be able to do in the future for your team
2. Write a short headline for the job function.
3. Do a brainstorm with current employees on what they think the job should entail. (They may have good ideas and insight. Use the good ideas they come up with and discard the rest.)
4. Use gender-neutral language and eliminate bias in the job description
5. Understand the values of the organization, and what behaviors will both fit with the culture, and what will add to the culture.

Remember we said – it's a partnership. If your company is using an Applicant Tracking System, great and beware. Great candidates can slip through the system if you are only selecting based on keywords, and this creates inequities and lack of diversity within your workforce and workplace. In our experience, it is critical to ensure your recruiter knows what you are looking for from a holistic perspective. Some of the best candidates can come from outside your industry, have educational and outside experiences that would be great for the job instead of specific work experience. Untraditional experience or jobs with similar skill sets may bring new and unique experiences to the team. Be open and when possible, look at the candidate's applications yourself, as things may be by-passed by the recruiter or Applicant Tracking System (ATS).

Build an interview team that is diverse. Have folks outside of your team or department interview for company values and culture fit. Beforehand, explain the job and role, what you are looking for, the skills and competencies you need on the team, the types of personalities that will work best on your team, and how you view the candidate as a culture match. Use interview guides to avoid redundant questions and answers, and ensure you debrief the interviews after all of the interviewers have met with and scored the candidates.

Ensure that you have your interview team recognize any biases they have going into the interview from the resume to the candidate's LinkedIn profile. We need to ensure that all bias is checked at the door, and everyone goes into the interview with an open mind.

Ultimately, you have the final decision... You are the boss! But do not disregard the input and feedback from your recruiter and the interview team. They bring in different perspectives, will eliminate bias, and can provide insights as to how this person will fit in the greater organization and culture.

Maybe you can build your own team, or perhaps you can hire a few new team members. What should you look for? You can't look just for competency (technical ability) alone, as you could be hiring a bad apple that will destroy the morale of the team. Look broader than skill set.

The 4-C's of Selection

1. Competency. One of the first things a manager thinks of when they must deliver results is whether a candidate has the competency to do the job. Do they have the skills, competencies, and/or expertise required to do the things necessary to fulfill roles and the responsibilities of the job?

This is both a natural and useful focus. However, many managers make the mistake of hiring their team members based upon this singular attribute instead of the additional three attributes below.

2. Conscientiousness. Of all the personality or character attributes, the one most useful to getting high performance is conscientiousness. Conscientiousness means that a candidate is thoughtful, careful, and considers the impact of their behavior on others. A highly conscientious individual who may lack some of the technical skills to get a job done and be trained in those skills. Once they are trained, their conscientiousness will drive them to do the things necessary to fulfill their goals. This is both satisfying for them, and incredibly useful for the team.
3. Cooperativeness/Collaboration. If you have a team that truly collaborates to get the job done, then you will want to assess their desire, willingness, and ability to cooperate and collaborate with others. If they are unwilling to cooperate and collaborate with others, then they may not be a good choice for your team. This depends on the unique situation of your team. We acknowledge that some workgroups are called teams, however they do not function as a team, as there are in fact few interdependencies. That said, all it takes is a person with a bad attitude to bring the overall team morale down and make folks resistant to giving their best effort.
4. Culture Add. The final consideration is 'culture add'. Many organizations say they use "culture fit" as a means for selecting the right candidate for the position. We believe that selecting for culture fit is problematic and can be seen as discrimination. For example, "cultural fit" means people who think similarly, and may share the same interests, or be

fun to be with and hang with. What if a candidate does not fit the "mold" and instead brings new experiences, different backgrounds, innovative, and forward-thinking ideas? By looking for "culture add" you are thinking about ways to grow the organization and focusing on ways to create a more dynamic, and future-focused organization.

Talent Development

First, and foremost, talent development is one of the top priorities of a people manager. That is *why* you are called a 'people' manager. People are your top priority! Without the right people with the right skills and competencies, you will not reach the goals set out for your team and those cascaded down the organization.

As a manager-coach, a key component of your job is growing and developing your talent. This comes in many forms and begins when your employee is onboarded. Yes, that is when we begin the talent development process by creating the Individual Growth Plan or IGP (see earlier chapter on IGP in this book). In the IGP discussion and your ongoing one-to-one coaching sessions a key focus is creating development opportunities to build the skills, competencies, experiences, and knowledge your employee needs to move ahead in their career. This does not have to be vertical or moving up the ladder. Growth and development can be horizontal – becoming a Subject Matter Expert on a specific topic, methodology, or subject - for example. Growth can consist of gaining a variety of different experiences across the organization, learning new skills, building different competencies, and helping your employee become more of a generalist. And for the ambitious, it can include moving up the ladder and building management and leadership skills. No matter what direction your employee chooses to take their career, you are a pivotal piece of this puzzle and their development.

Of course, training programs, stretch assignments, mentoring, education, conference attendance are all ways in which talent development is achieved. And your employee is taking the lead on what they want to do – and your role in their process, as the people manager, creates a foundation and support to move this forward.

Critical Conditions for High-Performing Teams

1. Purposeful Leadership

Projects and things are managed. People are led. Purposeful leadership gets better results. That fundamental definition means that psychology and sociology need to be considered in order to get sustainable high-performance. Activity comes after thought, and thought is always paired with emotion. Failure to attend to the whole person and the whole team will not result in high performance.

> *"Leadership is understanding people and involving them to help you do a job. That takes all the good characteristics, like integrity, dedication of purpose, selflessness, knowledge, skill, implacability, as well as determination not to accept failure."*
>
> Admiral Arleigh Burke

Let's understand that leadership is as much an art as science. What I mean by this, is that the number of variables that go into leading a team is so vast, that you can't always reason your way through it based on logic alone or follow a specific recipe like you would if you were baking a cake. Intuition and experience with other people and awareness of how they react to situations become significant tools to craft how you lead.

Being purposeful requires constant on-the-job observation of what is happening while maintaining an orientation to the near- and mid-term goals of the organization, the values and culture of the organization, and the capabilities of your team members. Looking only at goal-directed activity has a purpose to it, and it lacks the depth necessary to sustain success except with exceptionally compliant *Leadership*. You do not have to be the leader in all situations. In fact, it is best to hand off leadership responsibilities to others. The Navy has a concept of the Officer of the Deck (OOD), who is assigned to take control of the ship at times when the Ship's Commander is unavailable. The OOD is responsible for navigation and shipboard safety. In a similar manner, it may be appropriate to share leadership in situations such as when a subject matter expert (SME) can lead a meeting about particular topics, or if there needs to be someone in charge when the functional leader cannot be present.

BOOSTER CONCEPT

Constantly study the leadership strategies, tactics, and actions of leaders that you encounter, and that you hear about. Consider what you think is done right, and what can be improved. Reflect on what leadership tactics and strategies are purposeful, and which are impulsive. Then use that knowledge to look at yourself and what you can do to become more purposeful.

2. Common Goals & Stretch Goals

Common Goals are shared by all team members and are selected to make progress to achieve the Vision & Mission. Without Goals, the Vision and Mission are just good intentions. So, goals must be seen to be, at least in some way, quite directly impacting the Vision and Mission.

> *An example would be designing a unique regenerative-braking system for an electric vehicle (EV) in order to achieve the Mission of putting one million super-efficient EV's on the road.*
>
> *Goals can also seem remote from the Mission, for instance the accounts-receivable department of that same EV company has goals to increase the invoicing cadence to reduce outstanding collectibles by 3 days. Yet when one takes a "30,000-foot perspective," this goal also serves the mission of the company, since if it cannot collect on its invoices and sustain its cash flow, it will default on its debts and go bankrupt.*

Goals are both the "pull" to get things done, and the focus of accountability for collaboration. Team members should be able to see and understand how their own contributions to achieving goals affect other team members' abilities to get their own goals accomplished.

Selecting goals that drive relevant accomplishment is not that hard. Making them measurable may take a bit more thought, and you can almost always rely on three main measurables: money, time, and quality. Quality in this sense can be measured by the number of defects in product or service

BOOSTER CONCEPT
A team without a common goal is not that different from a group of people waiting for a bus: they want it to take them somewhere, and they aren't all going to the same place. Take the time to understand, communicate, and achieve buy-in to the shared common goal(s) of the team. This simple act does wonders for building coherence, congruence, and cooperation in your team. Develop a dashboard or scorecard so that all team members can see how their work is unfolding toward the goals they need to achieve.

Stretch Goals are compelling to the team. If team members possess skills and competencies to do a good job, then their "stretch" may be in getting it done faster. Teams that do not have compelling goals may flounder. They will likely produce mediocrity when they really need to excel. Consequently, it is incumbent upon the leader of the team to create and define compelling goals for the team, and to hold them accountable to achieving those goals.

Using the acronym SMARTER, you can set goals that are *Specific, Measurable, Achievable, Relevant, Timebound*, and then you will *Evaluate* how well the team has done in achieving those goals, and *Reset* the team based upon that information. Realize that just because you have a clever acronym for these goals does not alleviate a great deal of judgment and discernment. Use your team to think through and commit to creating compelling SMARTER goals.

BOOSTER CONCEPT
It is up to the leader to create SMARTER goals for the team and to motivate them to achieve these goals. That doesn't mean it happens all in your head. Be willing to hear how much your team thinks they can accomplish and to what quality. They

may surprise you with their ambition, or you may need to spur them on to do more than they think is possible.

3. The Productivity Plan: What Gets Measured, Gets Done

It is a truth of organizational behavior that what gets measured gets done. People simply respond to measurements. Whether it is their desire to avoid looking like a failure, or a fact that they need to compete, people will do what is required to meet their numbers. You've got to have a plan with metrics to make sure everyone is productive.

Establish KPIs (Key Performance Indicators) for each position. KPI's are the 3-5 most essential activities that should be on a **dashboard** to quickly see if the right activity is being performed and is "moving the needle" to accomplish team and organizational goals.

Examples of KPI's could be:

- Rate of production (units per hour, per shift, per day, etc.)
- Number of Customers contacted per employee/ hour/ day/ week, etc.
- Backlog of projects in dollar value
- Number of prospects in the funnel
- Profit-per-Project and/or Profit-per-Employee
- Accounts Receivables (total amount, avg. past-due time, # customers past-due, etc.)
- Number of Unique Visitors to website (each day, each blogpost, each connection-across other social media)

KPI's should be cascaded down the organization, so that they are directly related to the outcomes that the organization is striving to achieve. Make sure the KPI's are true indicators of the essentials, and not a confusing cloud of all the things on which an individual is being measured. In other words, keep them "key."

Measuring progress without celebrating progress is a loser's game. Make sure you celebrate!

BOOSTER CONCEPT

Build your "dashboard" to allow both team leader and team members to see how progress is advancing. We recommend that the leader establish a newsroom, where each team member's KPIs are updated daily. Some managers that we have worked with also use a simple red-yellow-green color-coding to indicate a degree of accomplishment based upon agreed-upon goals.

A "newsroom," a "news wall," can show the plan as a public dashboard that keeps everyone accountable to accomplishments. This should be reviewed at every team meeting. You can use a simple traffic light Red-Yellow-Green coding for things that did not get done (Red), things that made progress and did not get finalized (Yellow), and things that got done (Green).

4. Creating Camaraderie

There is an old maxim that states "there is no "I" in the word team. In one sense, this is true, in that each team member does have to sacrifice some of their own ideas and preferences to support the team. That said, people operate from their own self-interest, so it is up to the team leader to educate and enlighten team members on how members work with others to create "enlightened self-interest."

If there is to be camaraderie, then each team member must try to create it. This is much easier for those who are "people persons," and can be much harder for those who prefer technical work. So, it may take the "people persons" to initiate the building and sustaining camaraderie, and the "non-people people" must be open and participate in behaviors and activities that build team spirit.

Obviously, trust is central to team spirit. Many people mistake the idea of "good faith" with trust. Not to get too much into the weeds, but good faith is what we extend and expect from others, believing that if they are admitted to the organization, that they will be acting in good faith to make the team work. Trust, on the other hand, must be earned. Trust comes from example after example of behavior that fits the expected values of the organization. You cannot have camaraderie without trust. Trust, therefore, often takes time.

Shared adversity increases trust if team members show their ability to deliver on their promises to do things that support the team. Set your team up for success with smaller, more easily accomplished challenges. Break big initiatives down into very small tasks that can be accomplished. Make sure that each team member is delivering. Take time in your team meetings to recognize, appreciate, and celebrate small accomplishments and success. This invests in confidence and productivity that can be leveraged for increasingly difficult challenges.

Each team member must do their part to build camaraderie. That means that even the shy ones, the aloof ones, the arrogant ones, and the ones who simply do not quite care enough, all must do their part if the team is in fact going to have a good team spirit and build camaraderie. The more team members actively contribute to positive team camaraderie, the stronger the team will be. Just because some members do not wish to participate in this way does not mean that the leader should yield to those off-purpose attitudes. The leader has an obligation to build positive team camaraderie by holding all team members accountable for the behaviors that sustain great team spirit. Therefore, the leader must structure team activities so that all team members contribute to building team spirit.

BOOSTER CONCEPT

Have a rotating role on your team for a monthly Camaraderie Czar. Start with someone who would be a "natural" in the role to give the concept the best chance of success and momentum. Have a meeting with them to help them plan what to do to encourage camaraderie to give meetings more engagement and get one another to appreciate one another more: these could be icebreakers, special contests, after-work socials, or special moments and celebrations. Make sure the monthly Czar follows-through! Have them mentor their successor, and their successor picks their Number Two, and so on to keep rotating through so that everyone has this role, with support and encouragement.

5. Rules of Engagement (RoE)

Team members must know what acceptable and unacceptable behavior is. This includes things like being on time, respecting others, keeping others informed, and fulfilling deliverables. A team charter that specifically mentions the desired team behaviors and deliverables works wonders to make sure everyone knows the Rules of Engagement (RoE).

BOOSTER CONCEPT
Spend a half hour discussing and identifying "best practices" and "worst experiences on a team." Have each team member write down three Do's and three Don'ts for behaviors that will support the team in its mission and hinder the team in its mission. Then craft a list of the RoE on a flip chart, discuss what each phrase means, and then when everyone is on board, have them sign the RoE. This visible and public commitment to the RoE is a great way to apply some peer pressure to gain adherence to good, team-supporting behavior.

6. Communication Nourishes Teamwork

Communication is the lifeblood of teamwork. Both formal and informal communication are key to strong teamwork. Formal communications are task-focused updates to the team dashboard, emails, phone calls and meetings. Informal communication happens between meetings, before and after-hours whether on a break, walk back from a meeting, or over a virtual touchbase. The less that a team communicates informally, the more important formal communication becomes.

Good communication about work activity is candid, useful, accurate, and timely. Each team is different and has different needs, and the more frequent the communication, typically the better the productivity, and the less guesswork is involved.

Communication increases certainty and decreases mystery. In the absence of communication, people usually fear the worst. You, as the team leader, should determine how much informal versus formal communication is required to ensure your team's success.

BOOSTER CONCEPT
We recommend spending 10% at the end of every meeting making sure that you have a clear communication plan to assure that all stakeholders (outside the meeting) are clear on what is going on. Without clear communication, bad things (and wasted effort) usually happen.

7. Recognitions and Celebrations

A team will always have poor spirit and low engagement without recognition and celebrations. People want to feel valued, and recognition shows them they are indeed valued; these things also motivate people. Understand, however, that the form of recognition that is appreciated by each person can be different. Among the forms that can work to recognize achievements are public mentions of accomplishment, gifts, time off, plaques and trophies (even if non-traditional), personal thank you notes, time with the leader, special events.

Celebrations are shared recognitions, and can be as simple as thumbs up, shout-outs, "high-fives," pats on the back, and pics posted on social media. A culture that celebrates small progress as well as big accomplishments is more enjoyable and connected than one that only celebrates after crossing the finish line.

BOOSTER CONCEPT
Don't wait until the end of a project to celebrate. Do it while a project is in the making to keep motivation going.

8. A Path for Growth

How does the team get better? One member at a time.

How do the members learn and grow? Only with intention marked by action.

As the saying goes, if you are not moving ahead then you are falling behind. So there needs to be a structured plan for the team and its individual members to get additional training, education, and time to think about how to get better. These feed the need for growth and are valuable tools to become more confident and productive.

BOOSTER CONCEPT

All teamwork has natural pauses, and natural transitions from one activity or work-phase to another. Take these natural pauses or transitions to do a quick review of what went well, and what can be done differently to execute more productively in the next phase. These meetings do not need to be long-winded; 20 minutes can be enough to identify most of the opportunities and challenges. Make sure you write down these key insights, and especially look for gaps in training and skill development. Then make plans to fill these gaps as soon as possible.

THOUGHT STARTERS

- What about these 8 conditions resonates with you?
- What are 1-2 of these conditions you are looking to focus on, improve, or emphasize?
- How will you share these conditions with your team to build alignment?
- What will success feel like when you've embedded these conditions into your leadership style?

3

Aligning & Promoting Mission, Vision, & Values

A mission statement is not something you write overnight but fundamentally, your mission statement becomes your constitution, the solid expression of your vision and values. It becomes the criterion by which you measure everything else in your life.

Stephen Covey

The mission, vision, and values (MVV) of an organization lead the direction for (a) why the company exists, (b) what the company wants to become, and (c) how the company employees are expected to behave.

Senior leaders are the keepers of the MVV. It is their role and responsibility to ensure employees will have a clear direction and are aligned with that direction. When misalignment occurs, the success of the organization could be in jeopardy, as a part of the organization may be going one way, while another faction is going in a different direction. It's easy to see how misalignment can be devastating to an organization if everyone is working towards different goals. A senior leader plays an important role in sustaining alignment to the MVV. Without that direction and alignment to values, the organization will fragment and flounder.

You are thinking, "Great... I can do this!" But before we focus on ways to ensure your team and employees are connected and aligned to the mission, vision, and values, let's make sure we are aligned on the definitions of each.

Defining Mission, Vision, and Values (MVV)

Many definitions exist among business consultants for the constructs of mission, vision, and values. Based on the research and work we have done, the definitions below are very clear, concise, and easy to remember.

- **Mission**: Your mission is your company's purpose. It's why you do what you do. And it should stand the test of time. It lays out the organization's "purpose for being".
- **Vision**: A vision statement, in contrast to the mission statement, is a future-oriented declaration of the organization's purpose and aspirations. This is "what we want to become". A vision statement is how to accomplish the mission (measurable) and can also change over time. Leaders must continuously revisit it to ensure it still makes sense.
    - Company strategy flows from the Vision. Since the strategy is intended to achieve the vision and thus satisfying the organization's mission. The vision should make it easy to explain business decisions to employees and customers. It clarifies why the company is making a product /selling a service in a certain way.
- **Values**: Cultural values help you achieve your vision and define behavioral expectations. They explain **"how the company expects employees to work"** and the behaviors

associated with each value. They come to light when interviewing employees for the organization, and how employees are expected to act and behave as they do their work and represent the organization.

- With your company's values as their compass, employees will naturally work toward the company mission and vision.

Quick recap

- **Mission** is the purpose for being.
- **Vision** is what the company wants to become.
- **Values** are how the company expects the individual employee to work.

How the Mission, Vision, and Values Help a Manager

As a manager, you typically are not part of the creation of the mission, vision, and values and you are responsible for driving them down the organization and throughout your team. Therefore, as a manager you must at minimum be an advocate for organizational Mission, Vision, and Values, and at best you are a Champion for them. If your personal values do not fully align, then just as a defense attorney may provide dispassionate legal advocacy so that an alleged criminal can get a fair trial, you must act as an advocate for the organization. Of course, if you are fully aligned with your organization, then it is easy to be a Champion for the MVV. You can also use them to help you manage yourself and your team.

- The mission statement offers you a way to frame your own thought process, as well as a framework for developing your team's own mission, vision, and values, and can be used to shape the direction and focus of your team.

- The organization's mission statement, vision, and values help you act consistently. Not only do you know how to carry out your own job, and you are better able to guide your employees in their own duties to align with the company direction.
- The mission statement and corporate values will help you build and plan for your team. Company values and your team's own values play an important role in deciding who you interview and hire for your team. The mission statement can play a role in planning for future projects to ensure the project or initiative meets the company's goals. For example, if the mission statement focuses on developing innovative results for its customers, the manager understands the need for future projects to be different rather than simply rehashing solutions that are already available.
- Corporate values guide employees to make decisions when the optimal decision is unclear. In many ways, values act as organizational "DNA" that guides activity and strategy.
- Lastly, the mission statement can help you assess your personal performance and that of your direct reports to the company's mission. For example, if the mission statement emphasizes innovation and cutting-edge developments, you might assess the work of each employee to determine who is coming up with innovative and creative ideas.

It is very important to understand best practices in connecting our employees and ensure directional alignment to the Mission, Vision, and Values.

Connecting and Aligning Employees

It's great that the organization has defined and set into place the Mission, Vision, and Values and that is only the beginning. To keep these alive and to move them forward, the organization must ensure its employees are all working towards the same thing. There are a variety of ways in which this can be done. Below are some examples to help you get started and keep them front and center.

- **Engagement or Climate surveys**

  Roll out an employee engagement survey and ask alignment-centric questions about your mission, vision, and values. For example, include questions like "What is the company's mission?" Or "How do you contribute to the company's mission?" to get started. If you find that your employees' answers are inconsistent or inaccurate, you will need to help them better understand how to contribute.

- **Decision making**

  When a company outlines its mission, everything and everyone begins to head in the same direction. It becomes easier to spot what's working and what isn't – you begin to see outliers. For example, say a new program is having issues. Ask: Is this something we need to reach our mission? If it's not, it may not be something to focus on at this time. It could be put on the to-do list for later.

- **Company-wide meetings**

  To keep employees engaged, regularly share news about how the company is striving to reach the mission and vision. Not only is a well-informed workplace much happier and more productive, and this also helps the entire organization keep an eye on the prize.

- **Individual goals**

  Managers should meet employees where they are. By analyzing what the employee does, and how they help achieve the company's mission and vision, managers can make it more relevant to the individual. Employees who clearly understand their piece of the pie find more meaning in their work and stay more engaged.

- **Regular meetings with direct reports**

  Weekly or monthly status and coaching meetings help managers develop a good relationship with their direct reports. These meetings also help ensure an employee isn't out of alignment for months before it's discovered.

- **Difficult conversations**

  When difficult conversations have to occur, look to the company's mission or vision or values to steer your talk. For example, in a manufacturing environment, you might say: "Our mission revolves around quality, and people trust that about us. This week, there were several instances of poor-quality products being put out there. They did not meet our standards, and you have to understand the disappointing message this sends our customers." Sometimes you have the wrong person in the job, and other times, an employee just needs to have it brought to their attention. Ask yourself, "How can I connect these conversations back to our company's values?" This is a way to focus attention on how this person's behavior or lack of work efforts are disconnected with the company's core values.

- **Rewards and Recognition**

  Keep employees aware of how they're doing and reward them and recognize them for good work. For example, if client retention is important, it might mean rewarding an employee who did everything they could in a difficult situation to keep a client happy. Make sure rewards are linked to the mission and vision.

Your Mission, Vision, and Values play an important role as you grow your team, build your team, and develop your team members. Each of these concepts helps to recreate connections that support organizational integrity and congruence and to drive your business and reach your goals. And remember the importance of rewarding and recognizing individuals on your team, on projects, and within the organization; incentives in the form of rewards and recognition say so much about who you are and what your organization stands for.

Below is an example of **Saterman Connect's mission, vision, and values**. Look at your organization's mission, vision, and values and see how you can cascade it down to your function, department, or team.

> ***Mission statement:*** *To unlock your organization's full potential, beginning with your people.*
>
> ***Vision statement:*** *To create a world where company cultures ensure every person is seen, heard, and valued.*
>
> ***Values:***
> - ***Balance:*** *Well-being is the cornerstone of a culture that supports everyone and encourages engagement and fulfillment.*
> - ***Conscientiousness:*** *Understanding how your intentions will be seen, heard, and felt are the best route to positive impact.*
> - ***Courage:*** *Addressing difficult topics isn't easy, and courageous conversations can change everything.*

> - ***Growth Mindset:*** *Real transformation exists when you are open to new possibilities and accept that change is constant.*
> - ***Safety:*** *Cultural evolution and growth are only possible when people feel safe in judgment-free environments.*
> - ***Vulnerability:*** *Leaders who share their vulnerabilities connect more deeply with everyone in their organization.*

Develop Your Productivity Plan

Your organization may already have a planning tool that can get you organized. Your former direct managers may have tools that you are familiar with. We have seen innumerable plans over the years, and some are great, some are overly simplistic, and a great many are too complicated and require more work than they are worth. And of course, we have seen managers struggle to accomplish deliverables without any plan at all! Those were struggles that would have been reduced or possibly eliminated had they taken the time to build a plan!

Your plan should answer the following 12 questions:

1. Where are you going?
2. Why are you going there?
3. What are you solving for, and how does it contribute to organizational goals?
4. How will you identify and determine the steps and resources required to accomplish your goals?
5. Who are your partners and collaborators who carry your vision?

6. Who are the stakeholders outside of your team that our deliverables impact, and how will this affect them?
7. What are the must-do deliverables?
8. What are the challenges and hurdles that you must overcome to be successful?
9. How will you measure your progress?
10. How will you create a sustainable structure?
11. How will you learn from your mistakes and course-correct?
12. How will you reward and celebrate success?

Your direct supervisor may engage with you very directly in defining your deliverables. Or they may only give you a vague sense of direction. But know that your direct supervisor will still be interested in *"what did you accomplish in the last quarter?... ``And what are you going to do this next quarter?"* Having a clear plan to answer those questions places you among the better managers!

While companies love to lay out a multi-year vision, oftentimes you see shifts in the strategy along the way. The overall vision may stay true, and how the organization gets to that vision might change. How do those changes impact your role within the organization, and therefore, how do you intend to shift your productivity plan? Let's acknowledge that your team will be impacted. In what ways does that impact your team? How do you want to share those shifts with your team? What other shifts can you anticipate that will affect the team?

While answering the above questions is essential for constructing a good plan, the simpler you can establish the milestones and the KPI's, the more focused your effort will be. It can be easy to overthink your plan. Strive to keep it simple.

Simplicity can reveal problems with your plan. As a guide, if you can't explain it to an 8th grader, it may be too complex.

Make sure that your Key Performance Indicators (KPI's) are on-target to the things you need to accomplish. There is not necessarily a problem if they are stated as outcomes versus being activity based. That said, it is often a simpler preceding activity that is the more valuable KPI. For instance, you may want to reduce the percentage of customers with unpaid invoices over 60-days, on the way to the goal of reducing late (30-day plus) accounts receivables to no more than 2% of accounts. That could be a useful KPI. But on the other hand, it is really an outcome, and not a performed activity. A KPI based on an activity to reduce 60-day plus late receivables to no more than 2% would be the number of phone calls and letters made to delinquent accounts. By dividing the 90-day period into smaller segments (weeks or months), you will have a better idea how much to increase those customer contacts to get faster customer payment.

BOOSTER CONCEPT

We like a 12-Week/90-Day Productivity Plan, with the 4-week intervals to review your accomplishment on your most important milestones. The 13th week is a buffer week to complete final tasks. It is a "time-out" to review how things went as well as a way of providing planning days to prepare your next 12-Week/90-Day Plan.

Tools such as Gantt charts and calendars are hugely important in keeping everyone on track. A variety of apps provide these tools, and others, that provide different views of your progress. Find one or two and work on it. (None are perfect for everything...)

4
Onboarding

Alone we can do so little; together we can do so much.

Helen Keller, Activist & Teacher

Traditionally orientation was an introduction to the organization and a day of completing HR paperwork, and at some point, in the past 20 years, organizations realized that an introduction was not enough. Employees needed more time, information, and connections to be successful. That is when a new hire orientation was born, and paperwork expanded to include other important things a new hire needed. To be successful, new hires would benefit from being assimilated to the organization and culture, their team, and their jobs, over a period of time, and this best practice turned into the "first 90-100 days" on the job.

Today the world is more competitive, companies are fighting for great talent, and employees want much more from their organizations. This is where a planned onboarding process is imperative to assimilate new hires into the company culture. Organizations and their leaders (you) need to consider an onboarding approach that incorporates the role of the manager, not only in onboarding new hires, and also as part of the talent acquisition process to ensure new hires are successfully onboarded on Day 1.

Let's break this down so you can understand some key factors of Onboarding.

- It is imperative that the hiring manager along with Talent Acquisition supports the new hire through the hiring process from selection and interviewing, through acceptance of the job offer. This step is owned by Talent Acquisition, the Hiring Manager, and Human Resources.
- Company onboarding is, at the minimum, a 90-100-day process that fully engages and equips the new hire (also transferred/promoted employee) both professionally and culturally into the organization, the team, and their role. This is a step owned by Human Resources, IT, and the Hiring Manager.
- Job and functional onboarding are critical components in successfully integrating the new hire into the role and their team. This step is owned by the Hiring Manager, with support from team members and Human Resources.

The Argument for Onboarding

According to the Human Capital Institute's article *The State of Talent Management* (Campbell & Schweyer, 2008). There are five workforce challenges affecting organizations today:

1. Attracting and retaining skilled professional workers
2. Developing manager capabilities
3. Retaining high performers
4. Developing succession pool depth
5. Addressing shortages of management

Organizations are greatly feeling the impact of these five challenges especially in today's work environment. These challenges alone make the argument for a sustainable onboarding program that supports new hires transition into the organization, the function, the team and their job.

A few statistics prove this point: from a Society for Human Resource Management (SHRM) article: Hirsch, A.S. (2017). *Don't Underestimate the Importance of Good Onboarding.* Retrieved from https://www.shrm.org/resourcesandtools/hr-topics/talent-acquisition/pages/dont-underestimate-the-importance-of-effective-onboarding.aspx.

- 69 percent of employees are more likely to stay with a company for three years if they experienced great onboarding.
- New employees who went through a structured onboarding program were 58 percent more likely to be with the organization after three years.
- Organizations with a standard onboarding process experience 50 percent greater new-hire productivity.

Today's companies are building their culture strategy around talent development and retention. They are spending more time and effort on talent recruitment and selection and are creating robust onboarding initiatives that build new hire loyalty and faster assimilation into the organization, the team, and their roles.

Onboarding as an Organizational Initiative

Onboarding is a holistic initiative. We believe it begins during the interviewing process as the manager and recruiter are sharing company, culture, and job information with the potential new hire and providing insights into what it would be like to be a part of the organization. Official company onboarding begins once the new hire accepts the offer, and HR processes the paperwork.

New (recently acquired, transferred, and promoted) employees need to get up to speed and engage quickly to be effective. The onboarding phase, focused on increasing employee productivity and enhancing cultural assimilation, typically takes between 90-100 days, and begins with a Welcome to the organization from the CEO, an on-site or virtual company-culture onboarding program, support from IT and Benefits. Then the hiring manager takes over and provides a team and job function onboarding, along with training for the specific role.

We believe the hiring manager must be involved throughout the process, as it is the only way new hires will effectively assimilate to the organization, their function, their team, and their role.

Nettie's Story: Onboarding Goes Beyond, ON...

> *I have been a huge fan of onboarding for many years as I have experienced horrible onboarding initiatives and some great ones as well. What I realized as I started to design onboarding programs for companies is that onboarding does not start when the new hire steps through the door. And it's just not the first 90-days of transitioning into the company, the team, and the job, it encompasses the entire employee lifecycle... and we call it BeyondBoarding™.*
>
> *BeyondBoarding™ is an end-to-end talent develop-*

ment process that is a foundation of the employee lifecycle. It begins with 1) Pre-boarding: Creating a consistent message about your company's culture for sourcing, recruiting, and selecting new talent. 2) Onboarding: Culture assimilation for new hires into the organization, team, and job; identifying goals; creating performance growth plans. 3) Post-boarding: Focuses on growth and development opportunities; building engagement; increasing retention; fostering company talent ambassadors. For more information about BeyondBoarding™ visit ***Saterman-Connect.com.***

I am going to focus on the Pre-boarding phase as this is where I see companies failing.

BeyondBoarding™ begins when a hiring manager recognizes a new/existing position needs to be filled, who needs to be involved in the process, and what steps need to be taken before the job can even be posted. It begins with Talent Acquisition and HR. Let's start with the job description. It may be a new job so you must start from scratch, or it could be an existing job... These are all the things to consider. What is the job title, and does it track across the organization? How about the skills and competencies required? What are they and do they track with other positions like this? You get my drift... There is a lot to consider in crafting the job description. Now we need to ensure there is no bias in how it is written. As well as ensure the compensation is set against industry standards and is equitable. Once this step is complete and the recruiter is in alignment you are ready to post the position.

Next comes the interview process. What are the steps you will take, how many rounds of interviews, does the candidate need to do a presentation or create new code? And while you are figuring that out, who is going to be on your interview panel(s)? I always recommend a cross-functional team to do this. My biggest pet peeve when I was interviewing was to be asked the same questions from everyone I spoke with. This told me the company did not have their shit together.

Create interviewing guides to ensure you are gathering information from different perspectives. Assign different interviewers to ask questions about company values. And prep your interviewers. Ensure they know what you are looking for, who the candidate will interact with, and how the debrief will work. Explain to the candidate the interview process and how long it will take. And tell them who will follow-up with them and NEVER EVER ghost a candidate. It makes your company look bad. It is simple to send an email or make a call that they were not the right person for the job and thank them for their time. I have been ghosted too many times to remember. If that's how they treat candidates, then I'm glad I didn't get the job - and told friends and colleagues what happened, leading them to think poorly of those companies also.

Finally, ensure that between the time they get the offer and their first day on the job that you, Talent Acquisition, and HR take an active role in communicating how excited you are and create a feeling of belonging and inclusion even before they show up on Day One, either in-person or over video.

> *And of course, this should go without saying, create an onboarding plan and stick to it. This is what creates a true new hire experience that lets the new hire know you and the company care about them!*
>
> *We have shared many resources to help you in this process. Visit* ***SatermanConnect.com*** *to access these tools and templates.*

Onboarding Template

Overview: This template is a starting point to building your onboarding process, with the ultimate goals of embedding this into your organization. As you walk through the sections you will see that you start with the 'big picture' and then narrow down the information and tasks into smaller doable segments. Feel free to modify this in any way it works best for you and your organization. You can easily recreate it in Excel or Word.

Step 1: Identify Onboarding Objectives

(Identify the objectives you want to achieve with this initiative)

By the end of this initiative, new hires will be able to:

- Objective 1
- Objective 2
- Objective 3

Step 2: Onboarding Timeline

Create a timeline that is built off the objectives and takes into consideration the things that need to be accomplished from the time a new hire accepts the job – throughout their first 90 days.

- Week 1
- Week 2
- First 30 Days
- 30 – 60 Days
- 60 – 90 Days

Step 3: Identify Onboarding Team Roles and Responsibilities

(Identify the key people responsible for the onboarding process. Create a list that includes: Name, Title, Contact Information and what they are responsible for.)

[_____________ Name] [Title] [Phone]	Will provide ... (fill in)
[_____________ Name] [Title] [Phone]	Will provide ... (fill in)

Step 4: Craft the Onboarding Priorities List

The hiring manager is in the best position to ensure that the new hire's first experiences with the company are positive, valuable, and productive.

Its purpose is to help hiring managers prepare for the arrival and development of new employees.

To make onboarding a success, it is critical that Talent Acquisition, HR, and the Hiring Managers are involved in the process. The handoff between pre-arrival and onboarding can be murky. The involvement of these people/departments gives a new hire a positive impression of the company from Day One and throughout the end of their onboarding experience. Create the tasks to include pre-boarding, onboarding, and post-boarding.

Pre-Boarding

Identify the immediate actions needed to ensure your new hire is welcomed into the organization from the day they accept the job, through to other necessities, so they are operational on Day 1.

- Welcome Package / Portal Access from HR
- Welcome call/email from Hiring Manager
- Welcome by CEO (Letter or video)
- Benefits/other paperwork via email or portal to complete prior to Day 1

Key Stakeholder Meetings Template

Key Stakeholder Meetings are a process initiated by the new hire's manager that provides targeted conversations to support the new hires' assimilation into the organization. The goal of the meetings (within the first 30 days) is to help the new hire be more effective on-the-job and within the organization by providing advice, and feedback, and information. These meetings will provide insight and help the new hire's assimilation into the organization both formally and informally.

What is the Process?

The hiring manager invites key stakeholders including peers, direct reports, internal customers, and business partners to meet with the new hire. The purpose of these meetings allows the new hire to gather information to support their transition into the organization, their team, and their role. Some of the questions to be asked may include the following.

Sample Questions to Ask

1. What are the key skills and competencies needed to be successful in this job/organization/ team...?
2. What should I know about your organization/team?
3. Who does your team work with cross-functionally? Why is this important? How do you build that relationship?
4. What requires further focus for me to be completely effective?
5. What specifically do you need from me to support you/your team?
6. Who else do you feel I should speak with?
7. What key information do I need to learn to support you/your team?
8. What's your best advice for me?

Key Stakeholder List

[The purpose of this section is to provide the new hire with a list of stakeholders with whom they need to meet in order to be effective. If you are unable to list a specific rationale behind each name on the list, it will be important to spend time with the hire to help him/her prioritize the list.]

Senior Leadership Team

If appropriate, list members of the Senior Leadership team

- Name, Title (List 1-2 reasons why they are key to meet with):

1. ______________________________

2. ______________________________

Direct Reports

List the appropriate members of the Manager's team (i.e., the new hire's Manager and his/her direct reports).

- Name, Title (List 1-2 reasons why they are key to meet with):

1. ______________________________

2. ______________________________

Peers

List the appropriate peers here (i.e., the new hire's immediate peers or team members).

- Name, Title (List 1-2 reasons why they are key to meet with):

1. ______________________________

2. ______________________________

Key Internal Stakeholders

List the new hire's key internal stakeholders here. These should be the people that are most important to meet with during the first 30-60 days.

- Name, Title (List 1-2 reasons why they are key to meet with):

1. ______________________________

2. ______________________________

External Stakeholder

If appropriate, list any external stakeholders here (e.g., customers, partners, and vendors)

- Name, Title, Division (List 1-2 reasons why they are key to meet with):

1. ______________________________

2. ______________________________

Our 20 Best Practices for Onboarding

We can't leave you without a list of best practices for Onboarding, based on years of embedding Onboarding initiatives into organizations.

1. Fast offer and acceptance process.
2. Create an epic welcome and get the CEO, Hiring Manager, Team involved.
3. Get paperwork out of the way.
4. Get equipment and other resources ready, especially all the IT needs.
5. Share important first week information asap so there are no questions or concerns before the new hires first day on-the-job.
6. Assign a buddy or mentor.
7. Create a memorable first day... get new hires immersed in the company culture.
8. Create team building opportunities for the new hire to assimilate into the team and get to know each person.
9. Build a 100-day onboarding guide that includes: key contacts, important web links, company information, FAQs, important job information, individual development planning tools, learning and development links/opportunities... to name a few.
10. Plan a schedule for the first 30-days, and beyond. Help them establish a routine.
11. Schedule meetings with key stakeholders and team members within the first 30 days.

12. Meet early and often. Make time every day for the first two weeks to meet with your new hire at the end of the day to debrief and ask questions.
13. Share shifting goals to frame your Individual Growth Plan (within the first 30 days).
14. Get to really know your new hire - likes, styles, hobbies, family, and interests
15. Give your new hire the opportunity to get to know you - your style, communication preferences, and interests
16. Enroll your new hire into key training programs.
17. Discuss internal programs, opportunities… such as Mobility Programs, Employee Resource Groups (ERG's), Clubs, Wellness benefits.
18. Celebrate often and ensure the new hire is happy, engaged, challenged, and being heard.
19. Use an open-door policy to allow for conversations, feedback, and ideation.
20. Create a community within your team to build trust, collaboration, communication and fun!

Icebreakers for Onboarding

- **Basic Introduction**: Name, role, one thing that someone does not know about you.
- **Introduction with tenured group**: Name, Department, Tenure with organization, One accomplishment you are proud of.
- **Introduction for a team**: Name, Position/Title, What do you think your team does well.

- **Penny Icebreaker** (share historical info): Handout pennies with dates that are significant to your group (1990 – 2005).
- **Significant Events**: Each person shares a significant personal/business event from the date on the penny.
- **Timeline** along the wall (share success/history): Begin by pre-posting some significant company events on the timeline; each person posts three - five sticky notes with both personal and corporate events on various dates on the timeline.

5

Developing Your Team Members for Growth and Results

By failing to prepare, you are preparing to fail.

Benjamin Franklin

Creating 90-day IGPs with Your Individual Team Members

Take 30-60 minutes to share with your team members your journey in building your own growth plan. Remember, people learn by listening to other people's stories, so by sharing your own IGP and your vulnerabilities you are leading by example. This gives your team permission to share their own vulnerabilities and continue building trust. We know trust is earned in part through vulnerability, so leverage the growth plan as a way to build trust into your team dynamics.

Ask each of your team members to build their own 90-day IGP or growth plan in each quarter. This provides at least four times a year for a person to focus their development. This allows you to be a part of their journey in an authentic way. It also allows you to partner with them during your monthly touch bases to ensure you are inspecting what you expect. That's another 12 times a year (8 at a minimum) to check in with your team.

This type of diligence creates accountability. The goal here is consistency that allows for efficient and effective learning opportunities.

By building this mindful planning into your thinking, you are also exemplifying leadership and allowing others to watch as your team grows and thrives. Leaders are mindful, they are organized, they are intentional, and they know how to allow discipline to guide them versus stifling them.

Your team, or at least those that wish to grow on your team, will love this time with you so you can share development opportunities and create moments for growth together.

An example from Josh's perspective:

> *I was a Vice President and this emerging talent started working on my team. I immediately took to this emerging professional's passion, drive, curiosity, tenacity, and just plain hard work. One day she asked about the books I kept in my office. I asked her what she was interested in, and she just stared. I gave a slight pause to consider what she was thinking about. I was listening with my eyes to give her time and space to consider. Finally, she asked if there was something to get her started; something around leadership. I handed her The First 90 Days by Michael Watkins, one of my favorite business books. She smiled, ran off, and over the next few weeks she would share with me her learnings. I could tell that she was interested, and more importantly open-minded. Because she was my direct-report's direct-report I got to partner with my direct report. She too wanted to think about books she could read to learn more. You see, open-mindedness*

can be infectious in that brilliant way like a genuine smile (see the beginning of the book to capture that reference). What this woman demonstrated was genuine curiosity. You can't teach someone genuine curiosity.

Over the course of the next several weeks and months we built her growth plan together. Over the next 2 years, she was promoted (twice) and would finally end up at a different company in a more senior role. This woman is open, possesses a positive attitude, and genuine curiosity. Again, these are attributes you cannot teach.

One day about 18 months after I left that job, I received a text message. This message was from her father. To date, this is one of the most beautiful and magical parts of my career. It came during the 2020 Covid-19 pandemic; when lives, social injustice, and the world were disrupted in ways previously unseen.

In this text, this father celebrated his daughter. He shares the incredible hard work she has put into her career. In a world overwhelmed with gender inequities and biases, this father recognized the hard work she took to become an amazing businesswoman. He wanted to thank me for supporting her growth and for being a great mentor. She accomplished so much, and he simply wanted to acknowledge how incredibly talented his daughter is by sharing his pride with me.

My role as a leader was to support her, guide her when necessary, and watch her fly. I often felt that my most important role as a senior leader was to be a linebacker and clear the path for the leaders of tomorrow to run ahead and score as many

> *touchdowns as possible. This woman is an all-star running back. All I did was provide her the space to run, score touchdowns, and shine.*
>
> *One of the ways I supported her growth was through her growth plan. She was disciplined, owned the process, and created goals that she could accomplish over a specified time period. She shared her journey with accountability partners and myself along the way. She rose to the occasion.*
>
> *I did not learn this path alone or on my own. I had many people that showed me how to lead and deliver for my team. Mentors and great bosses that shared their versions of this 90-day growth plan approach. Paying it forward is crucial to becoming an impactful leader.*
>
> *To quote the television show The Mandalorian from the Star Wars franchise, "This is the way".*

Your teams are depending on you to show them the way and starting with a strong development or growth plan sets the tone for you to **Arrive. Drive. Thrive.™** as you build your career, your team, and your organization.

6
Delegating - The Secret of Great Leaders

The person who cannot be a good follower cannot be a good leader.

Aristotle, Philosopher

As a supervisor/team leader, you have many responsibilities; knowing how to delegate effectively and hold others accountable for delegated responsibilities is one of them, and it is essential. Realizing your full leadership potential and helping others reach their potential requires strong delegation skills. You must find opportunities to share responsibility and still ensure that the work gets done, both for you as a leader and for the professional development of your team members.

When done well, delegating responsibilities allows you to involve the members of your team in accomplishing important tasks, making their individual contributions more valuable; it also gives you the opportunity to focus on your leadership responsibilities, making you a better leader. Delegation benefits everyone.

What is Delegation?

***Delegation** is prioritizing your activities so you can appropriately assign tasks and responsibilities to others.*

Effective delegation means making choices about your responsibilities and then providing others with the well-defined direction, guidance, support, and authority needed to be successful.

Delegation means coaching and following up to ensure that results and standards are being achieved.

Delegation requires that the manager trust others and let go of control. Effective delegation means empowering, motivating, and developing team members to play a vital role in the organization's success.

Why should you delegate? Consider the following reason and ask yourself - "How might this help me be more effective and efficient in my role, and at the same time develop my employees?" Effectively delegating reaps the following benefits:

For you, as the leader, delegation:

- Gives you more time to focus on other tasks that only you can be responsible for.
- Allows you to complete critical tasks well rather than doing too much, poorly.

For your team, it:

- Improves productivity; more work can be accomplished.
- Increases efficiency; deadlines can be met more quickly.

For the employee, it:

- Allows employees to gain experience to take on higher responsibilities.
- Increases the level of satisfaction employees feel from doing their jobs.
- Provides employees with opportunities for development and growth.
- Fosters a greater sense of commitment and motivation among employees.

Delegating is not easy. As a leader it is hard to hand over responsibilities to others. We always think we do it better - We have the skills - We know the process - How could anyone do it better than me? However, if we want to be strategic in our role and have other higher-level responsibilities, we must delegate to create more time for ourselves.

If someone else does the job, perhaps they may approach it from a different perspective and still get the same results or even better results. As a delegator of tasks, you must ensure delegation happens properly. Just as significantly, the recipient of the delegated tasks must have the opportunity to contribute their insights and input regarding both the delegation process and the task itself - especially if you, the boss, could use the help.

There are two main reasons managers avoid delegating: Time and Trust. Let's dig a bit deeper into this. In terms of time there are two specific reasons managers avoid doing this: (1) They don't want to take the time to thoroughly explain the task to someone to do it; (2) Even if they are busy, they think it is easier to do it themselves.

Think about a time that you did not delegate a task even though delegating it would have saved you a great deal of time, effort, and frustration.

The second reason as mentioned is trust. You think you are the only person who can accomplish the assignment well. You lack confidence in your employees' abilities and experience, or you don't even know who you should delegate to. We all like to have control and when we delegate, we lose some control and therefore expose ourselves and/or the team or organization to risk, which could lead to fear of consequences or mistakes. Or lastly you don't know how to delegate. This is something that especially happens with new managers. Don't fear, we have a great model that will help the new experience manager identify ways to delegate effectively and efficiently and at the same time provide growth and development opportunities to your employees.

As you reflect on these ideas and principles, think about how you manage your time and prioritize your tasks and responsibilities. Explore your own delegation effectiveness and how you could more broadly share responsibilities and develop your delegation practices.

Remember, delegation is not about giving the tasks you don't want to do to others—nor is it just about giving yourself a lighter workload. It is an important leadership tool designed to help you be strategic and develop others.

Delegation Decision Framework

Let's begin with deciding how much you need to delegate a task or assignment. Consider the different developmental levels someone might be at and determine the amount of direction or oversight they will need using this decision framework. As you move from left to right on the framework, you will increase levels of delegating responsibility.

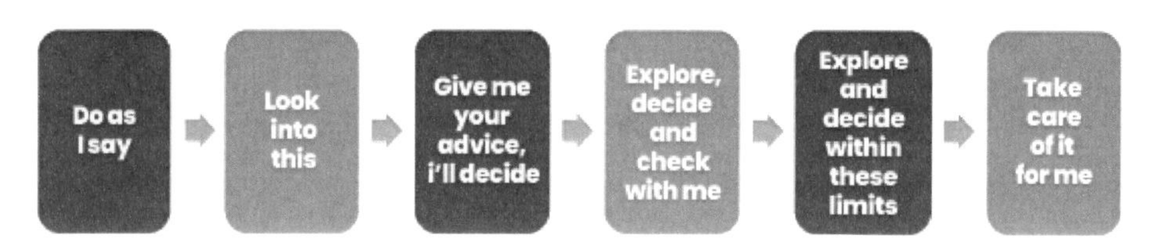

Delegation Framework © 2018-2021 by Nettie L. Nitzberg. All rights reserved.

Let's examine each of these in detail.

"Do as I say. *Here is the situation and what I have decided."*

- Impact on Control: You have total control over the delegation and the decision-making process.
- Impact on Your Time: This provides absolute control and also requires substantial time on your side.

"Look into this... *and tell me about the different options. I will then decide what you should do."*

- Impact on Control: You now trust the delegate to perform a thorough research which you can then safely use to make a decision.
- Impact on Your Time: You can spend less time on this, as the delegate will help you on the task. However, since you are making the decision, you will still need to go over the details and spend some time on the task.

"Give me your advice and then I'll decide... *and share my decision with you."*

- Impact on Control: You expect the delegate to provide recommendations, so you only have to use your intuition to confirm the decision rather than carrying the analysis yourself.
- Impact on Your Time: You spend less time on the task as you don't have to spend as much time on the decision-making process. However, since you retain control, if the need arises you can quickly take over and make sure the task is carried out with the right quality.

"Explore this issue and make a decision. Check with me… *before going ahead with the decision."*

- Impact on Control: You delegate the task and the decision-making, and still retain control in going ahead with a decision.
- Impact on Your Time: You spend only a small amount of time "signing off" the tasks. As you are relying heavily on the delegate for the analysis and the decision, you can save a considerable amount of time.

"Explore and decide within these limits. *I want you to solve this problem and consider the following parameters…. If you are satisfied, decide and go ahead with it. Otherwise, check with me."*

- Impact on Control: You now trust the delegate to research and decide so long as it is within the limits that you set.
- Impact on Your Time: Minimal time is spent by you mainly to define the task and set the parameters. You are holding the person accountable and have significantly reduced the amount of time needed on your side.

"Here is the problem. I want you to take care of it. *I trust your judgment. Here are the resources available for it. Do what it takes to solve it."*

- Impact on Control: You have given ultimate control over the task and the decision-making process. The delegate is now accountable and responsible for the outcome, and you have made this very clear. This is a high-level delegation and is usually carried out on strategic decision-making when delegating to people who have a high level of autonomy and control over their roles.
- Impact on Your Time: The impact on your time is extremely small. The delegation activity is carried out more as a consultation or a discussion on resources and how decisions could impact other areas of work as opposed to a straight-forward delegation activity.

Now that you understand the different levels of delegation and are able to determine where someone is in terms of their capabilities, you can use a delegation process to become effective at delegating.

Four-Step Delegation Process

Step 1. Organize & Prioritize

Key Points

- Create an inventory of your tasks, assignments, and responsibilities.
- Consider other operational activities or strategic initiatives that will contribute to your future success and that need time and attention.

- Prioritize your important and/or urgent tasks, responsibilities, and projects.
- Identify things to delegate that are developmental opportunities for team members.
- Evaluate what to keep, share, or delegate to others.

How To's

1. Brainstorm and create a list of your key responsibilities, tasks, projects, expectations, and commitments.
2. When building your list, consider:
    - New windows of opportunity.
    - Changes that need to be implemented.
    - Urgent needs and critical results that need to be achieved.
    - Areas where you or your team are falling short of expectations.
    - Ongoing assignments that are not getting done.
    - Things you don't do well.
    - Decisions and ongoing tasks that are consuming your time.
    - Tasks that are not your strength or area of specialty.
    - Assignments that you dislike or that disrupt your focus.
    - Activities that will provide employees with some variety in their work, new challenges, or opportunities for growth.
    - Tasks that will expose employees to career-enhancing experiences.
    - Work that will be improved because of an employee's creativity and special talents.

3. Refine your list by thinking about the responsibilities, tasks, and projects that will drive success for you and your team, and where you could reach new levels of success with some additional help. Ask yourself
   - What am I measured on?
   - What am I accountable for?
   - What are the essential deliverables that I must provide?
4. Review each item on your refined list and select a delegation approach by determining if it is something to Keep, Share, or Delegate using the guidelines provided in the table below:

Keep	Activities and responsibilities that you alone need to complete or that must remain your personal, primary responsibility.
Share	Activities or responsibilities that you can share with others by partnering with them to complete the task. (Be cautious that you don't always gravitate to this option, overextend yourself, or slow down the work of others.)
Delegate	Activities where responsibility and authority can be completely delegated to others, as long as the individuals to whom you delegate are appropriately monitored and held accountable for progress.

Cautions, Tips, and Obstacles

- Review and update your list of tasks, responsibilities, and projects on a regular basis. Make revisions to your delegation strategy when appropriate.
- Eliminate tasks that don't need to be done at all.
- Combine tasks that naturally fit together or can be accomplished jointly.

- Avoid keeping the best tasks and assignments for yourself. Enrich and motivate others by including them in good or fun tasks and assignments.
- Ask team members what they think you could delegate.
- Be creative; ask your peers what types of assignments they typically delegate.

Step 2. Select a Partner You Wish to Delegate a Task To

Key Points

- Analyze the task to determine the requirements you have for the partner.
- Evaluate potential partners who fulfill the requirements you identify.
- Ensure that the partner has the attributes necessary to be successful with the delegated assignment.
- Forecast potential challenges or obstacles that the partner may face and if he or she has the capacity to overcome them.
- Choose the person you think is the best match.

How To's

1. Ask yourself, "What skills, knowledge, and experience are required for the partner to achieve success with the responsibility, task, or project I want to delegate?" Create a list of requirements.
2. Generate a list of candidates who have the talents and skills needed to be successful with the responsibility or task. Consider the following areas when compiling your list:
    - Individual abilities and aptitude.

- Individual experience and background (transferable knowledge).
- Existing work assignments and workload.
- Development needs of the candidate.
- Individuals who have not had the opportunity to demonstrate their capabilities.
- Individuals wanting more experience, responsibility, and professional development.
- Availability or time constraints.

3. Evaluate each candidate's strengths and limitations and make a tentative decision.
4. Determine whether or not this responsibility or assignment will develop, stretch, or motivate the person you have in mind.
5. Assess the willingness and trustworthiness of the candidate you have tentatively selected and analyze any potential risks, burdens, or problems that you can foresee.
6. Make a final decision about the partner.

Cautions, Tips, and Obstacles

- Consider delegation opportunities for people with whom you are typically uncomfortable delegating.
- Don't simply delegate to those individuals who would perform the task or responsibility in the same way you would.
- Look for ways to match employees' career-development needs and plans with current delegation opportunities and situations.

Step 3. Communicate

Key Points

- Describe the task, assignment, responsibility, or project you want to delegate.
- Explain the purpose and importance of the assignment, as well as why you have selected him/her to be your delegation partner.
- Make sure the partner understands what he/she will be accountable for by reviewing all details of the assignment, including your expectations.
- Provide access to all the information and resources the partner needs to be successful with the delegated assignment.
- Seek a commitment from your delegation partner and motivate him/her to achieve extraordinary results.

How To's

1. Clearly explain the specific requirements and specifications of the assignment you are delegating to the partner.
2. Outline the scope of the assignment. For example, are you delegating the complete project or just one component of the project? Is this a permanent change in responsibility or a temporary one?
3. Identify key milestones and any specific measurements tied to successful completion of the task or project.
4. Communicate the level of importance and urgency of the assignment.
5. Help the partner understand the context or background of the task or project: who the customer(s) and/or stakeholders

are and how the project (and its successful completion) supports the team and the organization's success.

6. Identify any distinct expectations related to performance and outcomes. Explain the project deliverables, actions, behaviors, and results for which the other person will be held accountable. Discuss the potential consequences if these expectations are not met.
7. Provide the partner with the information, resources, and tips he/she needs to get started. Make sure the information you provide is consistent.
8. Help the partner forecast possible obstacles or barriers that he/she may encounter and, if needed, help him/her create a plan of action.
9. Describe the roles of any other individuals or functions involved in the assignment. Explain how they could potentially impact or be impacted by the delegated task or project.

Cautions, Tips, and Obstacles

- Explain the mission and goal of the project as well as the specifics of the task. Help the employee see the whole picture, especially the timeline.
- Be positive when describing the assignment or task.
- Clarification is your responsibility. Anticipate which parts of the assignment might need to be clarified and be prepared to do so.
- Whenever possible, delegate the whole job so the partner feels a sense of responsibility and invests him/herself completely in the assignment.

- Help others define and establish a priority level for the project.
- Be cautious that the assignment is balanced so the partner is not under-challenged or overworked.
- Help the partner understand why he/she is being asked to accept the assignment or responsibility.
- Delegate assignments as early as possible; waiting until the last minute to delegate a responsibility is neither fair to the partner nor to the task.

Step 4. Clarify & Support

Key Points

- Ensure that the partner has the appropriate amount of authority needed to complete the assignment.
- Continue to provide the partner with all the resources and information needed to successfully execute his/her plan of action.
- Let the partner know that you want him/her to succeed.
- Provide appropriate support so the partner is confident in his/her abilities and feels capable of fulfilling his/her obligations.
- Provide clear answers to any questions posed by the partner. Be patient and ensure the partner fully understands all of the elements of the assignment.

Now that you understand how to assess the fit for the person you are delegating to and the process to effectively delegate, let's consider the relationship between delegation and accountability. A leader holds others accountable by first clearly defining what the team member is accountable for.

Then, if those expectations are not met, the person is asked to explain the actions and decisions that led to that outcome.

It is important to remember that holding someone accountable isn't about punishment or placing blame—it's about discussing what happened with the person who is accountable. Being personally accountable is recognizing when our work will not meet expectations and communicating proactively about the actions and decisions that produced the result. Let's identify what accountability is and is not.

Accountability is:

- Being personally responsible for agreements and commitments
- Doing your best
- A communication tool when setting or clarifying expectations
- Ownership for more than just your part (results and outcomes)
- "Cleaning up" after a violation, and "owning up" after a mistake
- Being courageous
- Closing the loop
- Creating a culture for the team and organization

Accountability is not:

- Assumed or automatic
- Compliance, doing the minimum required, or getting by
- Easy to do
- Blaming
- Inconsistent, fragmented, or incomplete
- Guessing what is expected

Some people resist new responsibilities. A delegation partner's resistance to taking on a new responsibility or being accountable may be in response to a variety of situations, attitudes, and assumptions. Consider the following:

- The assignment seems to be a menial task
- The assignment falls outside their comfort zone
- The partner has a fear of taking risks
- The partner is fearful of change
- The partner has a fear of failure
- There is confusion about the requirements of the task
- The partner lacks self-confidence or doesn't believe that he/she is capable
- The partner is under high stress and pressure
- The purpose of the assignment is unclear
- They didn't have input in the decision to take on the assignment
- They mistrust the person delegating the assignment
- They are too comfortable with the status quo

- It is inconvenient
- They feel they are losing status, power, and/or influence

What does resistance look like? The following is a list of attitudes and behaviors that might indicate a partner is resistant towards a delegated assignment and is demonstrating a lack of accountability:

- Difficulty getting started
- Doubt (not believing it can be done or completed)
- Confusion about how to get desired results
- Pretending not to know
- Withholding information
- Shifting the burden or blaming others or circumstances
- Nitpicking credentials and experience
- Being withdrawn, silent, or giving one-word responses
- Using budgets, time, staffing levels, or other excuses to delay action
- Deferring key decisions to others: the boss, team members, the committee – as examples

When you are faced with this situation, think back to the decision tree and perhaps you may need to reassess where they are in terms of their capabilities, and consider the amount of help and support they need. This may also require a conversation and as the manager it is a great opportunity to coach, listen and provide feedback.

7 Coaching for Results

Coaching isn't therapy. It's product development, with you as the product.

Fast Company

Have you ever experienced the power of coaching? If so, how has coaching supported your development? What unique ways have you benefited from coaching? How has coaching differed from other previous leadership development experiences?

Coaching has been an important part of our career and has supported us in unimaginable ways as we advanced throughout our careers. Coaching opens different perspectives and ways to consider new possibilities in the moments of opportunity or complexity. Additionally, coaching allows us ways to discover and explore ourselves, our roles, our lives, and more with the support of a guide or navigator.

Before we focus specifically on coaching, we want to clarify the differences between being a mentor, sponsor, and coach.

- **Mentor**: a wise and trusted counselor or teacher; an influential senior supporter
- **Sponsor**: a person who vouches or is responsible for a person; a person who makes a pledge or promise on behalf of another

- **Coach:** someone who provides both technical and conceptual guidance to allow you to become more self-aware, explore challenges, and opportunities and with a result of better performance

Can you begin to see the differences based on the definitions? We hope so, as there are very unique roles the mentor, sponsor, and coach play.

Coaches provide a safe, supportive, and encouraging space to explore what is desired and how to achieve it. Coaching usually follows the interests and needs of the individual being coached. At times, coaching may focus on reflecting and clarifying aspirations and goals; at other times, coaching may focus on problem-solving around specific challenges; or, coaching may focus on finding motivation and inspiration to pursue goals; and finally, coaching may focus on accountability to activity that moves the individual forward toward achieving their objectives, which usually includes a component of growth and self-development.

Now, we are onto something. We are emphasizing these keywords above to ensure leaders start to differentiate and understand with more clarity the world of coaching. Coaching is about a safe, motivating, and goal-oriented environment. A coach is a partner, partial stakeholder, and definitely a navigator for the person they are coaching. Coaches don't have the answers, but rather, allow a person to self-discover and find the answers for themselves. A coach supports a person that wishes to explore what's behind new doors previously closed, pave new routes for personal growth, and illuminate areas within their lives that may currently be dark. So, while a mentor may provide advice, and a sponsor may vouch for you and/or be your advocate, a coach supports you by allowing you to explore, discover, and expand your own bandwidth on your own terms. The coaching journey always has objectives with deliverables that ensure goals are measurable and achievable while pushing a person's boundaries and limits to get at the heart of growth. Growth can be uncomfortable, and that's the power of having a coach to lean on and to push you. You are not alone as you explore "you".

We always recommend people consider having all three types of people in their lives: mentors, sponsors, and coaches. All three types of people are valuable in their own unique and necessary way. As a leader, you must feel comfortable owning your role as a coach. While you can also serve as a mentor, and certainly a sponsor too, there's nothing quite like being a great coach to empower and encourage your team's growth; both as individuals and as a unit.

Let's share the five key benefits to support the reason coaching is crucial.

Coaching:

1. Drives your own improvement around skill sets and behaviors needed for your personal grow
2. Establishes a confidential and safe space for you to deeply and explore yourself
3. Creates achievable goals by maximizing your superpowers (or key strengths)
4. Builds personal awareness while exploring what makes you successful
5. Increases your overall engagement levels and connection to your passions, values and goals

You now have a framework around the benefits of coaching. Let's press on.

You are a 'kick-ass' boss! You are doing a great job moving your business forward. Now comes the fun part: developing your team. Wait … What? To be a great leader, you need to be good at driving a business *and* growing your team? Yep, that's what we've been saying this whole time! Believe it or not, great leaders need to do both. While advancing through our careers, we have learned leaders' behaviors and actions absolutely mattered as much, if not more than, their business results. We've always loved growing and developing the people on our team and within the organizations we served. Whether as consultants or in-house employees, one of the most rewarding parts of our work is watching teams flourish, grow, and deliver great business results because they understand the value of their critical skills in conjunction with their business or industry acumen.

One of the most important things you must do as a people leader is to conduct frequent coaching conversations with your direct reports. We, your authors, speak to this all the time. We take this leadership imperative seriously, we prepare for these important discussions, and act on this religiously.

These meetings show your people that you care, and you are invested in them. Again, you, as a boss, are only ever as strong as your team. Investing in your team is a #1 priority.

We wanted to share a few tools to deploy when preparing for a coaching conversation.

1. Be intentional about the time you set aside to meet with individuals on your team. It might be 20 minutes each, or up to an hour each week. Ask your people what they need, and if you have an instinct to extend or ask for more time … do it, schedule it, plan for it … it will pay off dividends in the end.
2. Plan ahead and create a safe environment to have open dialogue.
3. Start with the development conversation. Chances are you will uncover the everyday work, deliverables, to-dos, and more when discussing someone's development initially. In fact, we would recommend separating the performance development conversation from the to-do list conversation.
4. Lastly, leave your own baggage and development opportunities for a different meeting. This meeting is not about you, it's about the person you are coaching.

To take this a bit further, and provide some additional tips, the following chart outlines five stages for having effective coaching conversations. We suggest you write these down, take some notes, and do a little bit of homework before starting your own coaching conversations.

Five Stages for Effective Coaching Conversations

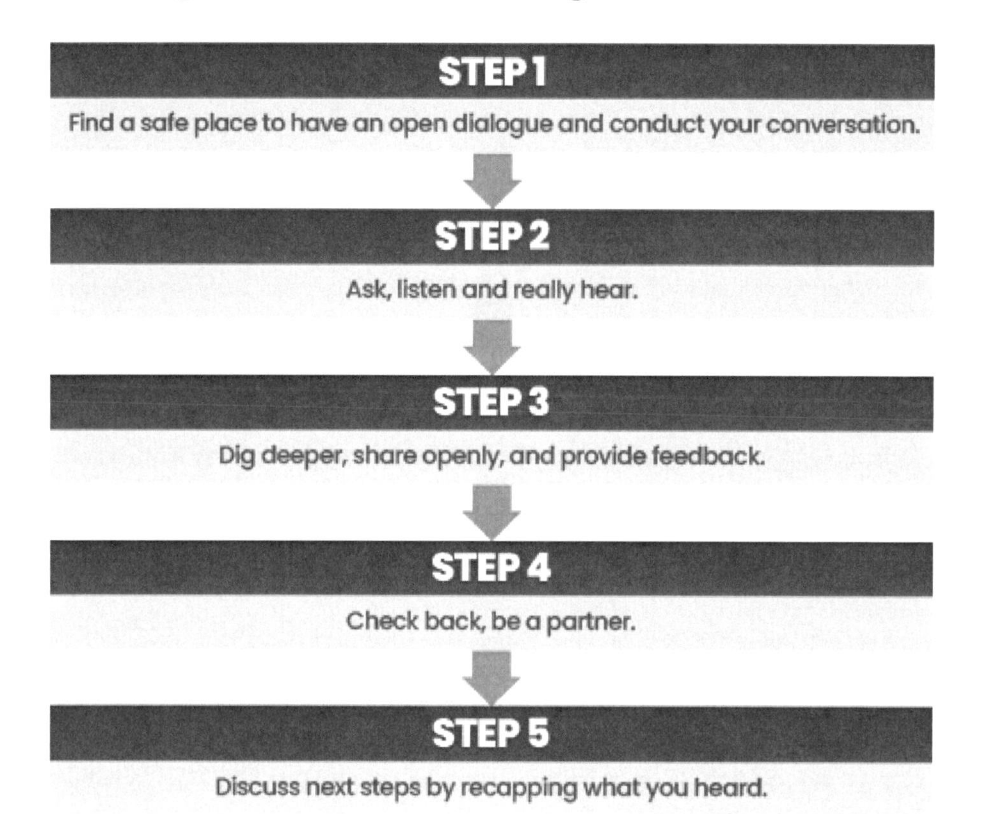

1: Find a safe place to have an open dialogue and conduct your conversation.

- Ensure you find a quiet place to sit, talk, and reflect during this growth and development conversation.
- Create an agenda for your meeting by asking the person you are coaching what's on their list of topics to discuss.

- This meeting is focused on their growth plan, which is very different from a recap or to-do conversation. Begin with their growth plan and, if time allows, discuss and support their work and to-do list. Chances are that their growth plan conversation will support their to-do list work as well.
- Be ready to remain judgment free.
- Ask questions as opposed to giving answers.
- Remember, growth for an individual is on their terms; you are a navigator who is supporting the journey *they* need to have, not the one you want them to have.
- Start the conversation by asking, "Tell me something good happening right now."
- Follow-up by asking, "What's one thing you wish you could change right now?"

2. Ask, listen, and really hear.

- Ask open-ended questions that start with the words 'What' and 'How'. Starting with these words allows you to have a conversation because a person cannot answer your question with a yes or no response.
- If meeting in your office, clear your desk, calendar, phone, and focus on the person you are talking to, so you are not distracted from hearing what they have to say. Ideally sit next to the person not across the desk.
- Take notes. These notes are important actions, development and growth ideas or plans for the individual and how you will support them.
- Use reflective listening to show mutual understanding as the conversation progresses. Reflective listening is mirroring the person's words to demonstrate how you understood what

they shared. Furthermore, it clarifies for the person their own thoughts that they shared with you.

3. Dig deeper, share openly, and provide feedback.

- Feedback is clear, actionable and provides someone with thoughts to consider for their future development or awareness.
- Simply saying you are "great" or "bad" without providing the Why's, How's, and What's doesn't allow them to clearly understand the behavior or skill sets they use that allowed them to shine or learn how to advance. Use examples citing specific behaviors and skills you have seen in action to help them grow. Try this as an example, "When I observed you doing A, I noticed you shone because of B." Or "When I observed you doing X, I noticed we have work to do together around Y to support your growth and leadership development."
- Give feedback that highlights positive things to continue doing, as well as opportunities to consider doing things from a different approach.
- Consider how your feedback provides support around their growth, development, and progress.
- Feedback should always be given with positive intent, even when the feedback might be tough to hear or tough to deliver.

4. Check back, be a partner.

- Being a leader means taking care of business. As a leader people are your business and they should never feel alone.

- Perhaps end by asking this question, "How might I support you?".
- Check back with your people on their terms. Ask for clear actions, next steps, and ways to support their development.

5. Discuss next steps by recapping what you heard.

- At the end of the meeting, have the person you are coaching recap what they heard, and share who is responsible for what happens next.
- Ensure each deliverable has clear next steps with timelines for completion.
- If a project, process, or initiative doesn't have a clear timeline for completion, create small action items together to ensure progress is happening, and will keep you both on track.

Hopefully these five steps and sub steps provide ideas and actions for your coaching conversations. You cannot drive business successfully if your team isn't engaged. According to many engagement surveys and polls, over 50% of people leave a job because of their boss. It's your job as a leader to help your team determine a meeting cadence that ensures engagement and supports their development and growth. As the individuals on your team grow, so too will the strength of your aggregate team.

Developing your team is the most important role you play as a leader. There's no set schedule for how often you coach someone. But meeting zero times with individuals on your team is never an option.

You have the very important responsibility of both driving your business and building, growing, and developing your people. But most importantly, you have the power and responsibility to lead your team to greatness!

There are some resources and tools to support you investing in your people that we always find useful. Books include:

- *The First 90 Days* by Michael Watkins
- *Helping People Change* by Boyatzis, Smith and Van Oosten
- *Tough Talk* by Becky Dannenfelser and Andrea Hopke
- *The Weekly Coaching Conversation* by Brian Souza

You can also find templates and tools like the one below at **SatermanConnect.com** to support your weekly coaching conversations.

<table>
<tr><td></td><td colspan="3">Coaching Tool: Your Toolbox</td></tr>
<tr><td></td><td colspan="3">This tool is a guide for anyone to look at the current and desired Skill Sets and Behaviors to support your growth and development</td></tr>
<tr><td></td><td colspan="3">Consider: What am I proficient in? What proficiencies are needed to be successful in my next path, position, area or function?
Who can be my partner(s) or hold me accountable to expanding upon or learning these tools?</td></tr>
<tr><td></td><td>Sharp Tools</td><td>Dull Tools</td><td>Tools I do not have</td></tr>
<tr><td></td><td>I am considered an expert; I could teach this tool to someone else.</td><td>I possess these tools; I am committed to working on sharpening these tools.</td><td>I want to have these tools for future growth and development.</td></tr>
<tr><td rowspan="6">Skill Sets</td><td>Example: I am great at Microsoft Excel</td><td></td><td></td></tr>
<tr><td></td><td></td><td></td></tr>
<tr><td></td><td></td><td></td></tr>
<tr><td></td><td></td><td></td></tr>
<tr><td></td><td></td><td></td></tr>
<tr><td></td><td></td><td></td></tr>
<tr><td rowspan="6">Behaviors</td><td>Example: I am a great listener</td><td></td><td></td></tr>
<tr><td></td><td></td><td></td></tr>
<tr><td></td><td></td><td></td></tr>
<tr><td></td><td></td><td></td></tr>
<tr><td></td><td></td><td></td></tr>
<tr><td></td><td></td><td></td></tr>
</table>

8
Communicating Progress

One important key to success is self-confidence.
An important key to self-confidence is preparation.

Arthur Ashe

Any time that you have deliverables, it's essential to communicate progress. How often you communicate about those deliverables is based on two dimensions: Urgency and Importance. The matrix below illustrates this communication concept based on the type of situation:

High Urgency **Low Importance** *Requires Occasional Updates* "Coffee for this morning's meeting"	**High Urgency** **High Importance** *Requires the Most-Frequent Updates* "Apollo 13 Catastrophe"
Low Urgency **Low Importance** *Requires Infrequent Updates* "Progress on Culling Inactive Files	**Low Urgency** **High Importance** *Requires Occasional Updates* "Building Next Year's Budget"

The Apollo 13 mission to the moon had a catastrophic explosion that leaked oxygen out into space. Without oxygen, the crew would die. The situation had extremely High Urgency, and High Importance. The engineers assigned to solve the problem by making workarounds had a countdown clock that gave them a deadline for success. And they gave constant updates on their progress to Mission Control, and to the spaceship so that the astronauts would know the state of their situation. They successfully found a solution through engineering heroics, and the astronauts returned safely to earth.

The best way to determine how frequently you should provide updates is to ask your own manager as well as your customers how often they would like to be updated about progress. And then, still over-communicate, because that gives people peace of mind. They can choose to ignore the over-communication, or they can also stay fully abreast.

It helps if you know the key metrics that people care about, including your boss and direct reports. You want to know the key info and data that is useful for your team to track. You don't need to give every detail: just the key metrics towards completion can be enough.

Having a way for your team to communicate to one another how their parts are fitting together to finalize the deliverables improves teamwork. Explore the numerous applications (apps) that can support you and your team in communicating, planning, and executing. All of them have one thing in common: they all work equally poorly if you don't use any of them!

9
Listening as a Leader

When people talk, listen completely.
Most people never listen.

Ernest Hemingway

Key Questions to consider before you read this next chapter:

- What are the attributes of a great listener?
- What does it mean to really listen?
- How do you like to be listened to?

Many engagement surveys have shown that most employees say they'd work harder if they were appreciated. (No shit, Sherlock!)

In trying to answer all three questions, common themes emerged: listening; being intentional; commitment to advocacy and acknowledging the barriers that might exist for true listening.

Let's remember that the work environment has dramatically shifted over the past several years. Even before the pandemic, many people and companies have shifted to virtual platforms. Listening skills have needed to shift accordingly. In this chapter we will share all the ways you can enhance your listening and coaching your team around best practices when it comes to listening.

We have two ears and one mouth so we can listen twice as much as we speak. This is also so we can hear all around us. The mouth is located on the front of our face so that when others speak, we see the lips move, the direction of the sound is pointed towards us, and we are able to interface with someone directly in front of us. In the virtual environment, this is even more important because it diminishes the non-verbal signals you can observe and hear. So, listening is both biologically and behaviorally driven, and an immensely important tool of leadership and teamwork.

A mentor of Josh's (Molly Langenstein) says, "Listen with your eyes."

People want to be heard. People are looking for safe and approachable connections. These real connections allow a person to start feeling comfortable sharing parts of themselves. Stephen Covey once said, "Most people do not listen to understand; they listen with the intent to reply."

We acknowledge some of the barriers to good listening: our body language, lack of time, patience, and lack of understanding or appreciation of someone's journey. Perhaps our concern over sharing our vulnerabilities can become a barrier. All barriers create walls that can be tough to break down. There are five pillars to really listening: eye contact, nonverbal communication, presence, mindfulness, and connection. These five pillars support creating safe spaces to deepen our appreciation and connection with people. So, whoever a person chooses to trust can start leading with understanding and a stronger connection.

We start becoming an ally to people when we stop talking and start really listening.

Listening deeply to others can require a complex skill set. That said, progress begins with one step forward, one momentary pause to ask ourselves, "How will I show up for this person?".

We must clear the roadblocks to listening before we can be in a place to really hear. Roadblocks might include:

- Distractions from your computer, tablet, or phone
- Complexities of prioritization
    - Example: Your boss needs something, your loved ones are calling, and your direct report has a meeting with you all at the same time. Sound familiar?
- Text messages are not an excuse. Put your phones away.
- What's on your desk? Clear the paperwork and make space to receive your guest or employee. Ensure people know that you are ready for their conversation.
- What's on your mind? Examples include:
    - A loved one is ill, or a child needs you
    - You had a fight with a loved one earlier in the day
    - You are excited for an upcoming meeting, event, or moment like a vacation

Active Listening – Ground Rules

1. Prepare Yourself to Listen
2. Eliminate Distractions
3. Be Ready to Focus (Stop Talking)
4. Listen to the Emotion

5. Reflect and Echo What You Hear
6. Demonstrate Patience
7. Acknowledge Your Unconscious Biases
8. Be Thoughtful When Asking Your Questions
9. Listen for Ideas – Not Just Words
10. Wait and Watch for Non-Verbal Communication

These Ground Rules can be expanded upon by exploring each one, asking clarifying questions that begin with What, When or How.

> *An example: Look at Ground Rules 3 and 8 and ask yourself – When do I talk? How much am I talking about versus listening to a conversation?*

Allow yourself the mindfulness to stop, ask yourself how you listen and give yourself some feedback so you can test, then try and pilot new ways to listen better in the future.

Let's explore some of these ground rules in further detail. If you are a really good listener, you can place your vulnerabilities aside and as a leader put a person's vulnerability at the forefront of your energy. This is another way of saying that you are not the most important person in the room when listening to someone else. They are — your attention should be on them!

Let us explore ways for you to empower your listening skills to allow you to become the best listener, leader, and support system for your team and people in general.

1. Get really good at non-verbal communication:

- Your body language is an important way to acknowledge that you are listening. Non-verbal communication such as nodding your head, making eye contact, your stance, hand, and arm positions, all can be used to convey active listening. This is key to allowing a person to feel safe, heard and valued. Giving people the proper time to share themselves is all part of being a good listener.
- Giving people the proper time to share themselves is all part of being a good listener. If you do not have the time to spend really listening to someone, perhaps steer them differently by offering them a new time to truly connect.
- What is the priority about the information you are sharing? Meaning, when you share feedback with a person, be clear and ensure they understand why you are providing the feedback you are sharing.
- Understand each of your team member's strengths ... What is their communication style? What is the way they like to receive, hear, share and explore information?
- Perhaps you utilize ***Gallup CliftonStrengths®***. (See Section 1 Arrive: Chapter 2.) Leveraging this tool is a great way to share your strengths, enhance communication and empower people to connect at a deeper level.
- Try one of these statements:
    - o "I really want to hear what you are saying and unfortunately, I'm late for a meeting. Might we find time to get back together so we can have a meaningful discussion?"

   - o "Right now, it is hard for me to really listen, and it sounds like you are sharing something important with me. Perhaps we can reconnect when we both have more time so we can have a thoughtful conversation?"

2. Ask thoughtful questions; ask action questions

- There's power in asking broader questions to give people the space to answer the question on their terms.
   - o "How can I support you?"
   - o "What is the role you want me to play in this conversation?"
   - o "What would feel like success at the end of our time together?"

   These types of questions demonstrate you are listening and really trying to understand a person who's trying to share something important with you.

Try using our three favorite powerful questions:

   - o "What motivates you?"
   - o "What does success look like? Or What will success look like at the end of "X"?"
   - o "How do you wish to be recognized? How will you celebrate your successes?"

3. Reflective listening shows you are hearing and understanding a person

- "I'm hearing you say this, "x". Perhaps even add, I'm looking to ensure I'm hearing you correctly. Please correct me if I'm wrong."
- "Is this what I'm hearing?"

- Ask, "What about this conversation is confidential?" Create a safe place for people to share openly.
- Ask, when appropriate, "How are you doing?"

Remember that whether you are in a virtual or physical environment, listening is vital. The approaches you take within either environment are key to your success as an active listener. How will you show up the next time someone in your life, whether in the workplace or elsewhere, needs you to really listen?

10
Giving the Gift of Feedback

We all need people who will give us feedback.
That's how we improve.

Bill Gates

What is feedback? The term 'feedback' is used to describe the helpful information or criticism about prior action or behavior from an individual, communicated to another individual (or a group) who can use that information to adjust and improve current and future actions and behaviors. Feedback occurs when an environment reacts to an action or behavior.

Effective feedback can be both positive and developmental; and is used to make important decisions. It is not always easy to give feedback, especially developmental or constructive feedback. Giving positive feedback should be easy, however we do not do this enough. Receiving feedback supports a person in becoming more self-aware as it highlights gaps, blind spots, and opportunities as well as strengths.

Most employees really appreciate receiving feedback, regardless of if it's positive or negative. Think about the last time you received thoughtful feedback. How did you feel?

How comfortable are you at providing feedback? Providing feedback is a key responsibility of a leader/manager. It is a skill that can be developed, especially if you believe in a growth versus fixed mindset according to Dweck, C. (2017), *Mindset – Updated Edition: Changing the Way You Think to Fulfill Your Potential*, Penguin Random House.

- A person with a fixed mindset is constrained by their beliefs and thoughts. They believe people are born with special talents and every person has different abilities and intelligence that cannot get better with time, persistence, and effort.
- A person with a growth mindset (thank you for the term, Carol Dweck) finds freedom in their thoughts and beliefs. They believe that people have special talents, abilities, and intelligence and these can be developed and increased with awareness, effort, and work. They take joy in the learning process – seeking new information and getting inspiration from others.

Some of the key differences between a **growth mindset** versus fixed mindset are:

- Talents, abilities, and intelligence can be developed through effort and practice
- Embrace challenges
- Persevere in the face of failures and setbacks
- Find inspiration in others success
- Accept criticism as a way to learn
- Look for people who challenge them to grow
- Focus on the process and learning without worrying about the outcome
- Leads to collaboration and innovation

Some of the key differences between a **fixed mindset** versus growth mindset are:

- Talents, abilities, and intelligence is fixed, it's who we are
- Avoid challenges
- Give up easily
- Feel threatened by the success of others
- Ignore negative feedback even though it may be highly relevant and useful
- Avoid new experiences with fear of failure
- Look for people who can reinforce their self esteem
- Can lead to cheating and deception

Carol Dweck's book Mindset (2017), beautifully sums up the two types of mindsets:

> *"When you enter a mindset, you enter a new world. In one world—the world of fixed traits—success is about proving you're smart or talented. Validating yourself. In the other—the world of changing qualities—it's about stretching yourself to learn something new. Developing yourself. In one world, failure is about having a setback. Getting a bad grade. Losing a tournament. Getting fired. Getting rejected. It means you're not smart or talented. In the other world, failure is about not growing. Not reaching for the things you value. It means you're not fulfilling your potential. In one world, effort is a bad thing. It, like failure, means you're not smart or talented. If you were, you wouldn't need effort. In the other world, effort is what makes you smart or talented. You have a choice. Mindsets are just beliefs. They're powerful beliefs, but they're just something in your mind, and you can change your mind."*

Everyone can benefit from feedback, and they also need to be open to receiving it. Effective feedback has benefits for the giver, the receiver, and the wider organization. Below are some reasons providing feedback is so important.

1. **Feedback is always there**: Every time we speak to a person, employee, customer, and vendor, we communicate feedback. It's impossible not to give feedback.
2. **Feedback is effective listening**: No matter the form feedback takes, verbally or via a feedback survey, the person providing the feedback needs to know they have been understood and they need to know that their feedback provides some value.
3. **Feedback motivates**: By asking for feedback, we motivate employees to perform better because they feel appreciated and valued.
4. **Feedback can improve performance**: Negative feedback is not criticism, it is constructive. It is given to help make better decisions and improve performance.
5. **Feedback is a way to keep learning:** Consider how feedback helps in one's development. Feedback is important across the entire organization to remain aligned to goals.

What are some of the typical behaviors you might see when giving feedback? "Positive feedback" is met with appreciation. "Negative feedback" is often met with denial, defensiveness, dismissiveness, or even a desire to attack the feedback giver. Why do people have these responses? Feedback that feels critical threatens the way someone wants to see themselves and the impact of their actions.

Overcoming that natural reaction is difficult. It's important to have a strategy, rather than just to try to "be nice." As a leader, you have an obligation to help people correct behavior that doesn't produce positive outcomes, as well as provide encouragement to help them learn and grow. You want to help the feedback receiver be clear about what they are doing, and how they can change to get better results.

Tips to be a better ***feedback provide***r:

Feedback DO's	Feedback DON'Ts
• Be willing to receive feedback yourself, and model being receptive to listening to how others would like you to change your behavior to get better results. • Make sure that you can stay cool, calm, and collected while you give your feedback. • If the situation is highly emotional, do let everyone cool down a few minutes, a few hours, or a day or more. • Be specific in describing what you have observed or heard. • Give the feedback as close in time to the observed behavior. • Identify the outcomes of their behavior that work, and the outcomes that don't work. • Be specific about what you want them to do differently. • Be willing to give positive feedback as encouragement. Again, focus on specific behaviors rather than generalized "good job!" type assertions.	• DON'T make assumptions about their motives. (Stick to observed behaviors and the observed outcomes of those behaviors). • DON'T make the feedback about their person, or their personality. (Focus on the behavior and avoid attacking them psychologically.) • DON'T wait to give feedback. The longer the time between an observed behavior and your feedback, the less the feedback (positive or negative) has any relevance. • DON'T use giving feedback to make others feel ashamed or hurt. • DON'T avoid dealing with negative behavior. Avoiding it undermines your leadership and sends a signal to everyone else that you lack the strength of character to handle tough situations. • DON'T use the situation as an opportunity to dump a bucket full of other concerns that you have stored away and haven't dealt with before.

We also recommend that you refer to the ***Five Stages for Effective Coaching Conversations*** in **Chapter Seven (7): Coaching for Results** for a more in-depth discussion of using opportunities to give feedback in consistently constructive ways.

Finally, we will pass a critically important concept that is absolutely **golden advice** for a leader:

"Praise in Public. Criticize in Private." In other words, give your constructive criticism/feedback only in private when it is between you and the other person. And heap praise in public when it is deserved.

Section 3

THRIVE.

Elevating Your Impact

1 Thriving as a Leader

Coming Together is a Beginning; Keeping Together is Progress; Working Together is Success.

Henry Ford

If you have performed all the activities that we discussed up to this point, then you will be well on your way to Thriving! Congratulate yourself, and bottle that good feeling!

On the other hand, perhaps you feel that you are not yet in the Thriving zone. If so, we suggest that you go back to the beginning of the book and examine each of the strategies, tactics, and methodologies that we have presented and find out which ones are particularly appropriate to use to get closer to thriving. Don't skip the hard work, as it's all important!

Remember, some important work to Thriving is developing *who* you are, not just your skillset to *do* specific work that any savvy manager should do. And thriving also means doing your work in a way that is sustainable with your drive, talents, and values. Let's be clear, you may be able to work 70-80 hours a week, and that may impact your ability to develop new skills and talents, or even to enjoy time with friends or family, much less explore new relationships. Denying yourself a full life to achieve work success is not really thriving.

Below we discuss additional ideas to help you sustain your ability to Thrive.

Thriving versus Surviving

Surviving is important. Thriving is elegant.

Maya Angelou

Conditions well beyond your control and influence can and will rise to create challenging situations. Sometimes, just surviving and keeping your wits about you is the best you can do. You will know if you are in one of those survival situations. You will feel the stress, answers will not be clear about what you should do, and you will not sleep as well.

Understand that it is just a phase caused by disruption, instability, and uncertainty, and you can---and will ---get back to thriving once some stability is achieved.

Here are examples of change that can bump you out of the thriving zone, and into the surviving zone:

- Your direct manager gets replaced. You are faced with a fundamentally new situation with new demands from a new boss and must go back through some of the steps in Arriving.
- Market conditions change, and therefore the company must change to adapt. You will likely have new goals and deliverables that you must Drive.

- Members on your team get reassigned or terminated. You may be back at a combination of Arriving and Driving with different team members.
- Your project gets canceled, and it is not clear what your new role will be, or what you will do. You must reset your Drive.
- You get reassigned, hopefully by promotion, and have a new department, function, or location to work in, with new people. You will have to Arrive all over again (and if you've followed our process, you will be in a much better position to get running more quickly!)

No matter what may bump you out of the thriving zone, three actions can help you to regain some equilibrium and get back on track to thriving.

1: Cultivate Resilience, Adaptability, and Persistence

Resilience means the ability to bend and bounce back. Rigidness is the opposite of resilience. Holding tightly to territory, positions, and even some ideas reduce your resiliency. In the short term, building resiliency is harder than doing it over the long term. That's because building resiliency is more about character than about being a task to achieve.

Nonetheless, to increase your short-term resiliency, the first thing to do is to gain perspective. Work to see your situation from a longer time span. Reframe your crisis as an opportunity to learn something new: about people, about organizations and how they work, and most especially about yourself!

Immediate resiliency can be improved by letting go of expectations, and the rigidness that comes along with it. (This is harder than it might appear, as most people are rather attached to their predictions of their future, particularly when it concerns their status, career, financial situation, and overall well-being.) But if you can let go of those expectations or loosen up your grip on those expectations, then you free up your brain to start solving problems instead of desperately trying to regain the past stability.

Adaptability can be cultivated by seeking out alternative ways of doing things. The old adage that "when the only tool you have is a hammer, you tend to see every problem as a nail" suggests the problems with lack of adaptability. To consider the reality that there are many ways to do things, just consider the multiple ways that one can cook a meal, or even one component of a meal, such as eggs. Learning how others do things in their own way illustrates how to identify when adaptability will work for you.

Persistence means not yielding or stopping, and to keep going. Persistence is what gave Thomas Edison the means to test over 1000 light bulb elements before finding a combination that was durable enough to put into production and lived long enough to be economically useful to a buyer. Persistence is what gave Michael Phelps the ability to swim miles each day in hard workouts that would propel him to Olympic records.

Where others might give up during difficult situations, persistent leaders move forward, they find ways to adapt, and overcome their challenges. Success takes time.

2: Manage Your Social Sphere

When the going gets rough, the savvy leader will reach out to their network! They work to strengthen loose connections and make new ones. In many ways, success depends more on "know-who" than "know-how." Reaching out helps you steer clear of the frustration and despair that can occur when the darkness of uncertainty falls like night in your corner of the organization.

3: Never Stop Learning

If you are not growing, you are dying. This is the simple truth of all biological entities, and especially humans and their consciousness. Times of disruption can often create wild new opportunities, and you should open your eyes to the potential opportunities during times of disruption. If you are managing your social sphere effectively, then you may not have to personally see new opportunities: others may see them for you. But you must keep your eyes and ears and mind open to recognize good ideas, no matter where ideas come from. Closed minds can't learn.

Here's an example: Your old boss gets reassigned, and your new boss may give you the opportunity to move into a new area you have been longing to explore. Whether you learn on your own, pay for private instruction, or get your new boss to sponsor you, the disruption can be a new opportunity to develop in new ways that are more satisfying and can increase your value to the organization.

And you can't get that opportunity if you aren't willing to learn and grow...or if you can't ask for it.

One particular skill that you may wish to develop is your ability to negotiate. This is a skill that includes analysis, reading people, and persuasion. It's a skill that can serve you in many areas of your life, and it may be particularly useful when your situation is in flux. Notice we're not saying to learn to be a negotiator; rather, to better develop your ability to negotiate. Any improvement can be of great benefit to you.

BOOSTER CONCEPT

Surviving is day-to-day. Thriving requires a longer-term view. If you are buried in the day-to-day, then turn for perspective to those who are older, wiser, or "interested outsiders" to help you get the perspective to elevate your game to build a thriving experience.

THOUGHT STARTERS

- What are you planning to learn right now?
- What are the ways you love to learn?
- In what ways can you inspire your team to learn?

2
Networking – Internally and Externally

If you want to go fast, go alone.
If you want to go far, go with others.

African Proverb

Making connections with other folks in your organization is always a good practice. It can help you understand how the whole organization works, it can open doors to new opportunities, it can even be a way to make new friends. And it should be pursued with some regularity.

You might even go back to the Arrive section within this book and look again at the Matrix of your social sphere. Perhaps, it is time to update it. You should see that you have opportunities to network.

Here's how to do it:
Start with an analysis of your internal network: Who are the most important /critical people that can influence your success and that of your team? How influential are you with them? How close are you with them? See what you can do to get some time with them and begin bringing them into your inner circle. (Be realistic: the CEO may be critical for your success, and it could be a stretch to get them into your inner circle. However, you

may be able to have some slight engagement with them and find out the company challenges that they see in the future.) Understand that this process will likely be more of a campaign of events and moments that can take months or even as long as years with some. It is not a one-and-done process. So, be patient with internal networking.

Next, identify two people from departments outside your own that you would just enjoy getting to know. Maybe they've posted something on the company website about their hobby, or an event they attended. Ask them about it. Engage in conversation. Just casually get to know them, and you will eventually get to know who they know. You never know where that might lead!

Finally, ask if you can set up a regular monthly meeting with your manager to discuss where you are, how you are performing, and what you can do to advance yourself, both from a personal and a professional aspect. These "campfire talks" can do wonders to make sure you know what your manager is most concerned about, and in helping you find ways to address those concerns.

In addition to networking within your organization, it is always smart to network externally with those in your industry...and even those who are in other industries! You never know when such connections will be advantageous, such as when you are recruiting talent for your team, when you want an industry-insider perspective, or when (perhaps) you yourself decide to explore the job market!

Nettie's Story: The Importance of Networking (or NetWeaving)

> *It's important to reinforce the value of networking. I love the concept invented by Bob Littell in his book "The Heart and Art of NetWeaving". Bob says, "NetWeaving is all about connecting others and*

acting as a generous resource for others because you genuinely believe in the law of reciprocity and that what goes around, comes around. You also believe that, when you open the door for someone else, you never know who YOU will meet as a result. Think about this: by offering your resources you are connecting those folks with someone within your Trusted (Value-added) Resource Network. This builds trusted relationships." (B. Littell, 2003, The Heart and Art of NetWeaving, NetWeaving International Press).

Since I (Nettie) began thinking about networking as NetWeaving I have created so many connections with people who I would not typically interact with. They have been a tremendous resource not only for me and for friends, colleagues, and even strangers. I have gone so far as to connect new people that moved into my neighborhood or met at a meeting with a doctor, hairdresser, plumber, and friends. If you have never moved your household from one city to another, you do not know how hard it is to find these connections not only for yourself and for your family. And, by the way, my number one ***Gallup CliftonStrengths™*** *is WOO - aka Winning Others Over. So this story speaks to me leveraging my top strength.*

Not networking is a huge mistake! You will be more successful at work as you meet people across the organization. But do not limit yourself to only internal networking. Making connections outside of work is beyond valuable. Just think who do you know in your network that can connect you to a great resource, a new hire, or even a future job!

BOOSTER CONCEPT

Learn more about networking! Three great books are a classic *How to Win Friends and Influence People* by Dale Carnegie and *Captivate: The Science of Succeeding with People* by Vanessa Van Edwards, and *The Art and Science of NetWeaving* by Bob Littell.

THOUGHT STARTERS

- How do you know when you've made a meaningful connection?
- In what ways do people support you getting your job done?
- What are the most significant pieces of feedback you've offered someone?
- What are the most significant pieces of feedback you've received?

Great Icebreakers for Networking

Mix and Mingle Bingo

- Object is to fill in as many names as possible on the bingo board
- Find "Bingo" squares you have in common
- Write their name in the matching square
- Each player can only sign another player's card twice
- There will be prizes awarded for the most signatures

Sample Bingo Sheet

Born in the same state	Have vacationed in the same place	Members of the same association
Have seen the same movie	Same favorite subject in school	Have eaten at the same restaurant
Use the same toothpaste	Speak the same foreign language	Have the same pet (i.e., cat, dog)
Have a relative with the same name	Have read the same book	Play the same instrument
Same favorite dessert	Went to the same college	Same number of siblings

To support networking within your organization, explore these Icebreakers and more (like Saterman Connect's "Get Connected Experience") by visiting **SatermanConnect.com**.

3
Letting Your Team Shine

Talent wins games, but teamwork and intelligence wins championships.

Michael Jordan

A central part of thriving is having others who support you, encourage you, cheer for you, and willingly contribute to your success. That means that they feel good, not bad, about working with you and for your projects.

Someone who feels betrayed that they did all the work while you took all the credit will not be a raving fan and will likely work on ways to undermine you. Let's face it, if you take credit for work you didn't do, you're a jerk. It's just that simple. Give credit where credit is due.

How do you let your team shine, and promote them?

1. **Talk about "we".** *We, the team, did the work. We, the team, faced the challenge. We, the team, stuck with it. We, the team, found the answers.*
2. **In team meetings, recognize and celebrate** with the proverbial pats on the back for the progress being made. Recognize that sometimes failure is progress because it

can tell you what NOT to do. Attend to the mental health of your team members by showing your appreciation, gratitude, respect, and even your admiration for them and their accomplishments.

3. **Praise in Public, Criticize in Private**. If a team member needs corrective conversation, make sure you do this in private. There are few things more humiliating than being criticized in public, among peers or higher ups. Using your position of authority to call someone out just makes you look like a bully, and others will not trust you because they will be wondering if you will do the same with them. This is a great way to lose support if you are foolish enough to indulge yourself.
4. **Publicly recognize the contributions of others.** Make sure you don't leave anyone out, no matter how small their role. Speak for them. Brag about them. Point out their unique contributions. You don't need to exaggerate. Just make sure you mention their name.
5. **In non-public settings**, meaning in casual conversation with your peers and other managers, **brag about the good things that people** in your department are doing. Talk them up. Words will get back around to them, and they will feel good that you are promoting them.
6. **"Don't steal the spotlight."** When making a public presentation, let your team members speak up about specific parts of their work that they accomplished, especially in their area of expertise. You may need to coach them about how to do that, as they may be unfamiliar with public speaking. In fact, it's a good idea to have at least a quick huddle and a script about who is going to say what, and for how long.

7. **Work to develop your team member's capabilities.** If you get a reputation for developing people who can be promoted to other roles, you become more valuable to the organization. Another way to look at it is that if you can develop someone to be as strong as you to do your role, then not only does that say good things about your abilities, and it allows you to be promoted without leaving a hole.

When you do these things with and for your team, they will support you. They will respect you. And they may go out of their way to work hard and help you Thrive even more!

BOOSTER CONCEPT
To quote President Harry Truman (1945-1953)**: *It is amazing what you can accomplish if you do not mind who gets the credit.***

THOUGHT STARTERS

- How do you find value in lifting-up your team?
- What are the best ways someone once recognized you?
- What are the different ways your team likes to be recognized?
- How often do you ask your team, "What does success feel like when we ...?"

4 Creating a Winning Culture

It's better to have a great team than a team of greats.

Simon Sinek

You should have confidence that your plans and your team's plan will achieve useful goals for the organization. If you are at all uncertain of this, then you need to have a re-alignment with your manager. Perhaps something got lost in translation. Perhaps conditions changed after the original goals were set that now give you concern that your plans are off track. Perhaps your manager mis-read what you and your team can accomplish, or what the overall organizational goals really call for.

You and your leader need to be on-point, on-track, and aligned with the mission and vision and values by achieving clear and congruent goals.

Once you and your leader are aligned, the next issue is how well you and your team behave in ways that are congruent with the values of the organization. In other words, you must actually walk the talk so that you are working with integrity.

If you do not have stated organization values, then go to the web and research the values of other highly successful companies. Adopt the best, then adapt as you need to fit with your own situation.

Do NOT just wing it. The easy path is seldom the best path. Think like a champion and do the work that will yield championship results.

Critical conversations may be required to confront discrepancies or gaps in behaviors and stated values. For instance, your organization may state that they cherish diversity and inclusion, and then it promotes only one perspective and actively disdains or even punishes people who think differently. You may have a difficult time living with this sort of hypocrisy. It can create a dilemma for you: on the one hand, you support the mission and goals of the company, on the other, you disagree with this sort of mono-cultural attitude that you feel is both oppressive and works against the overall well-being of the organization and impedes its mission.

Make sure you model the values you say that you believe in. Don't be a hypocrite and rationalize your behavior by diminishing those with contrary beliefs, so long as they perform as good team members in terms of their productivity and their direct behavior towards team members and cross-functional contributors.

The savvy management guru Peter Drucker said that a team will live up to or down to the expectations that the leader has for it. Therefore, never compromise on your standards for behavior that supports a winning culture.

BOOSTER CONCEPT

Impress on each person that they contribute to a great culture. Define what a high performing, fulfilling culture acts like, and then ask each person what they will do to contribute to make it happen.

THOUGHT STARTERS

- What are the differences between winning and succeeding?
- In what ways are people learning from their successes equally to their mistakes?
- How would you keep your team winning over time?

5
Maintaining Integrity

The ultimate measure of a person is not where they stand in moments of comfort and convenience, but where they stand at times of challenge and controversy.

Dr. Martin Luther King, Jr.

Sometimes it's much easier to see the holes in another's integrity than stay true to our own. Or to see the gaps between how someone else would handle something and how we would handle it. Other people's behavior can be a wonderful mirror for seeing our own, and we must be willing to look in that mirror and scrutinize our own behavior. That is why humility is such a useful character trait, and self-awareness is such a powerful tool.

Without being insulting and basing this observation on almost one hundred combined years of working with leaders, managers, and professionals of all types, we must be brutally honest: most people are not honest with themself and will more readily see the speck of dust in their teammate's eye than the log in their own. Self-awareness is both difficult to do, and difficult to accept when we do not see anything but wonderfulness in ourselves.

But this book is not written nor intended for the average person. This book is intended to lift those who wish for greater things, who are willing to push themselves harder than others, who know that to do more they have to become more. We want to elevate those who understand that the more integrity you have, the better things that will come to you, and they will come honestly, unencumbered with strings that tie you down or corrupt you.

And so, knowing what you value and having the integrity (courage) to stand for that becomes a real tool for life satisfaction. If you have matched your values to those of your workplace culture, then you will be in good standing.

BOOSTER CONCEPT

Every morning, look at yourself in the mirror and tell yourself you will do your best to maintain your integrity. This will give you courage when your integrity is tested. And then, every night, look at yourself in the mirror and ask if you let your integrity slip, and if so, redouble your efforts to maintain it. Your integrity, once lost, is very hard to recover...and the only one guarding it is you!

THOUGHT STARTERS

- Think of a time when your integrity was at a fork in the road. How did you know which path to take?
- In what ways might you inspire your team to continue leading and choosing the path of integrity?

6
Handling Office Politics

Teamwork is really a form of trust. It's what happens when you surrender the mistaken idea that you can go it alone and realize that you won't achieve your individual goals without the support of your colleagues.

Pat Summit

Let us be clear about what office politics is: The largely unavoidable natural tendency for human beings is to try and get their way and build their status, power, and potential through alliance-building, cunning, and self-promotion. NOTE: Confirmation bias could keep you from seeing the reality of office politics because you don't want to see it, or, making you think there is more politicking than there really is because you have bad chemistry with some people.

The question is not whether there is any politics in your workplace, but how much and how bad. Many workplaces have a general sense of unity and a system for promotion and compensation based on merit. Most people want to get along with others. Most people to some degree will subvert their own interests to be solid members of the team in support of team accomplishment. Let's understand that these people engage in garden-variety politics.

Though few compared to the great majority of folks you will encounter, there are toxic people, narcissistic people, and people who just can't help but put their own interests first and foremost. People who love drama, and will stir the pot just to get it. People who will be nice to your face and stab you in the back or talk dirt behind your back. And people who are just so desperate and unfulfilled that their own better judgment will not stop them from doing bad things to others to save their own skin, or to advance their status. Avoid these people at all costs. Get them out of your workplace if you have the authority. If you work for one, either strategize how you can work around them, expose their behavior to higher ups, or make plans to exit the organization.

Once we understand that "garden-variety" workplace politics does occur, the issue becomes how do we live with it? Here are some ideas:

- Watch out for rumors by checking for truth. Do not assume that whatever you hear from others is the reality. If you've ever played the child's game "telephone," you will know that unless you hear something straight from actual participants, then take everything with a grain of salt. And if the rumor suggests bad things, then make sure you check its truthfulness (remembering that even in times of stress, even actual participants may not have heard or seen things correctly).
- Be aware of unhealthy competition and use actual competition to propel your growth. Unhealthy competition usually leads to more desperation and cut-throat activity. Healthy competition can be talked about openly. You may be in competition with someone who has more drive, time, and talent than you. Or you may be that person who knows

you will do better than others. That doesn't mean that others can't "win" also. Healthy competition drives everyone to do better, to perform at their best, and to win.

- Lead with an open mind to the differences of others. Show that you are willing to be inclusive to those who are different from you and allow them to feel a sense of belonging. Not only would the world be boring if everyone was like you, it would also be unproductive. Others have abilities and talents that you don't have, and they are packaged differently. Their interests, style, and even their choice of friends and partners may not be your cup of tea, and that does not lessen their capacity to contribute.
- Turn disconnects into opportunities for enhanced communication and connection by focusing on your company values, team productivity, and shared aspirations. We call this finding the North Star that is a shared stable point that you can use to navigate even a ragtag group of odd people. Even the members in the land of misfit toys had a central rallying purpose that made them bond together to achieve their success.
- Find support when you feel all alone or isolated or are having to deal with stressful workplace relationships. This is the value of friends and family outside work. A coach, a mentor, or perhaps even someone that you do not know well and that you admire may be a source of perspective and support.
- Sustain strong communication by being aware of how others communicate. Listen, watch with your eyes, pay attention to patterns. Many people just want to be heard and understood. Sometimes they do things to get attention, and this can look like office politics when it is just a cry for belonging. Communication is the lifeblood of teamwork,

and without it, all sorts of rumors and bad actions can occur. Be a strong communicator by being a strong listener.

BOOSTER CONCEPT

Office politics is a fact of life. It can work for you, and it can work against you. Just know, however, that the more intensely the game is played, the more intense the reactions. Jockeying for position is inevitable, and when it becomes toxic, it's time to reconsider the risks and costs.

THOUGHT STARTERS

- When was the last time corporate politics served you? how?
- In what ways does corporate politics hold you back?

7 Finding New Opportunities to Deliver Value

Don't let the fear of striking out hold you back.

Babe Ruth

Hard work, on the business and on yourself, are both key to maintaining the journey in the Thriving zone. It is possible that you have a natural inclination to work more on developing yourself than you are inclined to just "get the work done," and both activities are necessary in the journey of managerial leadership that results in life in the thriving zone.

Having a realistic perspective on thriving is also essential. Being in the thriving zone can only last so long, as change is constant. Change disrupts predictability and routines that allow you to make plans and consistently perform at high levels. Change requires agility and adaptability, combined with a mindset of resilience to roll with the tide.

Your chances of thriving, therefore, rely on continuous improvement: stepping up your game as a guard against complacency.

It's better to create your future than wait for it. Being in a continual state of creation means that you have greater potential to stay thriving. Yet this does not mean continual dramatic creation, just continual creation, some of which may be dramatic and substantial, while a good deal may be small and incremental.

How do you stay sharp and creative rather than sticking with the status quo?

No business is ever complete. Opportunities abound for improvement, refinement, expansion, streamlining, speed, and quality. To spot those opportunities, talk to others about their frustrations, and open your mind to see these opportunities. Ask them what they would like to be different. Ask them what they would like to have more of, less of, none of. Don't accept their answers as the right thing; look deeper for other actions and activities that are the root cause, or the second- or third-order downstream consequence.

The real challenge is not finding opportunities, for there will be many. The true challenge lies in deciding where to put your precious time, energy, and resources so that the improvements are of value to your manager and your organization. Choose those opportunities that really help the business rather than those that end up being just busy-ness

Almost every business has its cycles or seasons of intensity, pause, and re-set. Noticing this pattern, how can you get ahead of the cycle? How can you interrupt an organization's pattern of procrastination? Or their pattern of over-thinking with little valuable return?

Use a large visual tool to get perspective on your year. Put pages for all months of the fiscal calendar on the wall. Place them as linearly as possible. Now go to work marking out all key days, weeks, seasons that will affect the people in your organization. Mark out the traditional school year. Mark out the winter holidays, and the summer vacationing season. Mark out key industry conferences, financial reporting dates, tax season, budgeting season, performance review season. Mark out all holidays, the company picnic and banquet. Mark out the Superbowl weekend, and March Madness. Mark down all the time that new products are released, and even dates that may be important for your competitors.

Now, step back and look at it and ask: what resources need to be dedicated at what times and in what ways to get the best outcomes? Small increments can make a big difference. For instance, one company took 4 months to complete their budgeting. One-third of the year the managers were at least partly distracted with budgeting, rather than being productive. This naturally caused a great deal of waste, as well as competition for resources. This could have all been done in one month at most, and possibly in one week if they made a real commitment to it.

To get an eyeball on future problems, use the wisdom of those who have gone before. What dysfunctional patterns have they seen? What low-hanging fruit for improvement has gone unharvested, or the seeds unplanted? What gaps need to be closed, bridges built, processes perfected? The ones who have been around may know something, and they stopped complaining about it because nothing ever seemed to change!

The U.S. military strategist Col. John Boyd (1976) said that the process of human acting occurs through what he termed an OODA loop: Observe, Orient, Decide, and Act. Of those phases, the Orientation step is always the most important, as it informs you about what is important. Without Orienting to the key values, any decision can be sensible, and yet 100% wrong for the situation.

So, when looking ahead, make sure that you orient possible changes to what really, truly needs to happen to make the organization more efficient, more on-point, more vital, and more profitable. A simple way of doing this is to work from the hypothesis: One year from now, if we make this change, what will happen to each and every other part of the organization and the people in each of the departments? If all you can come up with is positives, then dig deeper, as you may just be fooling yourself, and "pride goes before the fall."

To protect themselves from the insidious cancer of groupthink, some teams incorporate a "13th member." This is an arbitrary number; the point is that one member serves as a devil's advocate and can only argue against whatever the group is proposing. This tactic forces the group to confront its blind spots and tamp down irrational exuberance about their own brilliant decisions. It is a powerful tool to avoid stupid decisions born of not enough critical thinking, and arrogance.

BOOSTER CONCEPT

Sometimes the best ideas come from unexpected places. So, keep your ears and eyes tuned to see good ideas elsewhere that if put in place will help your team achieve more. And look for gaps that haven't been bridged (or haven't been bridged well-enough!) Opportunity abounds, if only you will seek it!

THOUGHT STARTER

- How are you ensuring each meeting has advocates, influencers, and naysayers to consider the perspectives needed to make an informed decision?

8

Being Smart About Sharing Your Vision

I firmly believe that when you have a foundation of respect, love of what you're doing and a shared vision, so much is possible.

Kerri Walsh

You may very well have formed a vision for how your team can most productively give value to your company. Or it may be in the process of being formed. Whatever the case, don't go blabbing about it to everyone you meet until it is ready for a reveal. Premature exposure can be embarrassing, and even a career killer.

Instead, make sure your vision is on track. Share your vision with colleagues, friends, and Subject Matter Experts (SME's) to seek their perspectives. Do not assume that you are the only one with good ideas and intentions to make positive change happen.

As you engage in conversations, you will gain a better understanding of who will be your allies or champions and support your vision. This also builds buy-in so the people you leverage can also serve as advocates in delivering your vision.

Consider as you socialize your vision:

- Who will be the active and passive resistors?
- Who will sit on the sidelines and spectate?
- Who will be willing to support you and move your vision forward?

You will gain understanding of the challenges of your vision. Examples of challenges might include: timing, personnel, resources, or executive support. This input is necessary when preparing to share your vision plan. Without this sort of information, many good vision plans have fallen flat. There is an axiom in the military: "No battle plan survives its first contact with reality." Be aware that just because you have created a great plan does not mean it will simply unfold the way you expect it to. In the end, before you share your plan, you will have to make a "business case" for your vision.

BOOSTER CONCEPT
Check your vision with others. Expect skepticism and criticism. Take it and learn from it, and use it to make your vision better, stronger, more compelling.

THOUGHT STARTERS

- In what ways are you sharing your vision plan?
- How are you ensuring your social sphere hears your vision (and you are hearing their vision for their function or area)?

9 Building the Business Case

71% of executives say that employee engagement is critical to their company's success.

FastTrack360

Since businesses measure success most easily by profit, the most central and enduring value of concern is "how can we improve profit?" So, to justify an improvement project, it can't just be a "good idea." It must have real value, or why bother? This need to show "proof" of real value means that you've got to think through all costs, and all potential incomes to find the value- the way that profit will be improved. This outcome becomes your business case for the improvement opportunity. It is best if you can boil it down to numbers: "If we improve process A by B percentage, we will save C dollars, resulting in a bottom-line improvement in profitability of X amount for the year"

It is beyond the scope of this book to walk through how to justify a change. Yet, simply knowing that you must justify that change is the first step in getting a green light to make the change happen.

It is not enough, of course, to identify a problem or an opportunity. You must also come up with a realistic plan to make the change and calculate the cost of making the improvement. It makes no sense to engage in a process that requires more of an expenditure to make the improvement than the value that the improvement yields! So, before you get too far, make sure you can make decent projections about the costs versus the return.

A good plan will include:

- A statement of the problem to be solved
- Why the problem should be solved
- What positive return on investment (ROI)
- The costs (money, time, personnel, opportunity costs)
- The phases, stages, and steps to reach the goal
- Who will perform what deliverable with the delivery date(s)

A good plan worth sharing will be approved before it is presented. That means that you have already lined up your direct supervisor and any senior leaders above your manager that will support you. Unless you are extremely confident and comfortable with risk taking, consider it foolish to pitch a plan without at least critical senior leaders already lined up with their endorsement. Do not feel or conclude that we are saying to meet with everyone before you launch your plan. Rather, consider the key people that will encourage you moving forward with your plan and therefore be your partner in delivering results.

BOOSTER CONCEPT

An effective business case can be explained in 1-3 simple sentences. Strive for cogent conciseness. Simplicity does wonders for comprehension.

THOUGHT STARTERS

- Ask your team, "What does success look like?"
- In what ways can you ensure you take the time to celebrate successes and learn from them to emulate the best practices and learn from any gaps?

10 Aligning Cross-Functional Teams

I can do things you cannot. You can do things I cannot. Together we can do great things.

Mother Teresa

Should you be in the position of needing to work with a cross-functional team to achieve your goals, you will need to make sure you are in alignment with the scope or measurement of the project goals. If you are the manager at the top of your function, then it is your responsibility to address this directly. If you report to the manager of the function, then you will have to address this indirectly.

Directly, you will want to engage with the top manager(s) of the other function(s). Generally, this works out reasonably well if you can agree on the goal, and the process to get you there. The key is making sure that you all understand that for the project or activity to be a success, that you are forming a new, larger team, and will need to be unified in that regard. If you are not aligned as a single team (for the purposes of accomplishing the project) then there will be serious problems.

We have found that two alignment stages are necessary:

1. An alignment of the top stakeholders,
2. An alignment of the team members.

Aligning top stakeholders is a prerequisite for aligning team members.

For each alignment, you will have to define, in written terms, the charter for the team, just as you did for your own team projects. It can also be useful to define the activities from each function that can either "Help" or "Hinder" the success of the project. Getting this information out in a transparent manner goes a long way to helping everyone know how to make the team work better.

An absolute essential for any team is a structure and agenda for communication. Communication is the lifeblood of teamwork. Without it, the team will flounder, or end up in mediocrity or failure. Taking the time to define the structure and agenda for each type of meeting is crucial for a smoothly running team.

Team meetings should be frequent enough to move the project forward without having to spend time just going over what was said in the prior meeting. In general, top functional-area managers should have a weekly meeting/update, while team members should have a daily scrum. The top manager's job is to smooth out unexpected wrinkles so that the work is getting done on-time, on-budget, and to-quality.

A solid and useful team agenda can be boiled down to these bullets:

- What needs to happen?
- To what quality?
- What resources are necessary to get the work done?
- Who will do it?
- By when?
- What other decisions need to be made?
- Are we on schedule & budget?
- Who needs to be informed about what is going on, by when, and by whom?

Never leave a meeting without a communication plan in place if there are stakeholders not in the meeting who may be affected by the activity of the team.

BOOSTER CONCEPT

The key to managing cross-functional teams comes from treating the group as a team. And that means getting everyone on-board, on-mission, with clear deliverables and accountabilities. Make sure that the leaders of the functional teams are fully aligned. If the team is aligned, and the "siloed" functional leaders are not, then you will have a difficult time creating unity and achieving your desired goals.

THOUGHT STARTERS

- How do you ensure cross functional teams are continuing to share openly?
- In what ways can you ensure each functional area shares their goals and motivating factors for success?

11
Managing Your Own Development

Every accomplishment starts with the decision to try.

John F. Kennedy

When thinking about your own development it is important to decide what you want to do, where you want to go, what makes you happy, then create and execute how you can get there. This exercise provides a step-by-step process to put those thoughts to paper and to really assess what you want to do, what you like to do, what you are good at doing, and how this helps you develop your personal development roadmap.

You can do this exercise on your own, with a partner, or even with your manager. If completing it on your own or with a partner, it is imperative you share and discuss this with your manager. It will help them to support your development.

My Dream Job

1. Current: Draw a picture of where you are today.
2. Future: Your fantasy job.
    - If you wave your magic wand – you will be working in your "dream job"! What would that be?

3. Why did you select this? What about it appeals to you? Identify the reasons you selected this.
4. Pair up with a partner:
    - Explain your dream job and why you selected it. Switch and repeat. (3 min each – 6 min total)
5. Now take three minutes and describe back to your partner: (Switch and repeat)
    - What you heard about the job that was exciting to them.
    - Skills or knowledge they need to have/have to do this job.
    - Why did you feel it was "their dream job?" (Consider this in terms of personal needs and professional development, if applicable.)
6. Individually take a few minutes and think about what you heard your partner say. What resonated with you? And why?

Where You Are Now...

Part 1: Today

1: Who are you?

- Take five minutes and complete the first section
- Regroup and share

Who Are You
[Use adjectives and descriptions to describe yourself: i.e., problem solver, people manager, being creative, making an impact, partially process oriented]

2: Education/Employment

- Complete this on your own.

<table>
<tr><td>Education

Degree:

School:</td></tr>
<tr><td>Previous Employment
• Company/position
• Company/position
• Company/position</td></tr>
</table>

3: Values Exercise

- Round 1: Go through the list and identify those values that resonate with you.
- Round 2: Go through the list again and eliminate identify the top 10
- Round 3: Now cut it down to the top five
- Round 4: Paired Exercise, Define the five values in your own terms by pairing up and explaining your top five values and how you would describe each one

This is an example of the values worksheet. The complete Values exercise worksheet can be found by visiting **SatermanConnect.com**.

Selection	Value	Definition
	Achievement/ Success	
	Challenge	
	Diversity	
	Empathy	
	Growth	
	Power	
	Strength	
	Teamwork	

My Values [From the Values exercise insert your values into this section of the Career Plan]

4: Limitations

- Take a few minutes and consider your personal limitations. Write them down.
- Regroup and share

Limitations [Describe your limitations]

5: My Current Position

- Key responsibilities.
- Key skills/knowledge to perform the job:
- What is your background and/or experience that led to this job?
- What do you like most about the job?
- What do you like least about the job?

My Current Position Title: Key responsibilities:
Key skills/knowledge to perform the job:
What is your background and/or experience that led to this job?
What do you like most about the job?
What do you like least about the job?

6: Five Year Goal Position

- When you look ahead five years, what is the position you imagine yourself in? [Perhaps it's your fantasy job.]

My Five-Year Goal Position is to:

7: Today to Future

- Compare your 'current' job answers to those of your 'dream' job.
- What did you identify as skills/knowledge in your dream job that are similar/same in your current job?
- What about your background and/or experience can be transferred to your dream job? Where are the gaps?
- What similarities do you see in what you like most about your current job, and the appeal of your dream job?

CONCLUSION

Throughout our journey, we have learned so much about leading teams, working with people, and finding ways to get better every day. The journey to becoming a great leader is ongoing, ever present, and never about perfection.

Arrive. Drive. Thrive.™ is all about remembering that you are an individual. You are part of a team. You are also part of an organization.

Whether you are just getting started, or reminding yourself how to reclaim critical skills, lessons, and hallmarks of a leader — you are not alone. Even we, the authors, are guided by these lists, tips, templates, and tools every day.

Keep going, growing, and motivating yourself and your team. People are the force driving business through innovation, creativity, ingenuity, inspiration, and execution.

Create your 90-day growth plan. Initiate that first feedback conversation (even if you are afraid or unsure about how to proceed). Practice listening for an entire meeting and do not ask one question or speak until the end. Explore ways to get uncomfortable — because when you are uncomfortable you are growing. And while growth can be hard, when you look back — **you will celebrate your wins, learn from your losses, and build a stronger foundation for your leadership to Arrive. Drive. Thrive.™** Oh, and don't forget, we (your authors) are here to support you along your learning and leadership journey!

***"Don't settle for mediocrity.
Be an active participant in your own leadership journey.
Empower your leadership."***

Gerald Hutchinson, Nettie Nitzberg, Josh Saterman

REFERENCES

SECTION 1: ARRIVE

Chapter 1: Arriving as a Leader

Sinek, S. (1992) *Start with why: How great leaders inspire everyone to take action.* (Portfolio).

Durant, W. (1926). *The story of philosophy: The lives and opinions of the world's greatest philosophers.* Simon & Schuster.

Srivastava S., John OP, Gosling, SD, & Potter, J. (2003). Development of personality in early and middle adulthood: set like plaster or persistent change? *Journal of Personality and Social Psychology. 84* (5): 1041–53.

Chapter 2: Deploying Your Strengths and Talents

Ratanjee, V. (2021). *Why managers need leadership development too.* Retrieved from www.gallup.com/workplace/328460/why-managers-need-leadership-development.aspx)

Gallup Inc. (2021). *CliftonStrengths®.* https://www.gallup.com/cliftonstrengths/en/home.aspx

SECTION 2: DRIVE

Chapter 1: Building Your Team

Major, R. (2017). *Jumpstart new leader and team effectiveness through the NLA Process.* LinkedIn. Retrieved from https://www.linkedin.com/pulse/jumpstart-new-leader-team-effectiveness-through-nla-robert/)

Chapter 3: Onboarding

Campbell B. & Schweyer, A. (2008). Human Capital Institute. Retrieved from https://www.shrm.org/resourcesandtools/hr-topics/organizational-and-employee-development/documents/hcilibrarypaper_79300.pdf

Hirsch, A.S. (2017). *Don't Underestimate the Importance of Good Onboarding.* Retrieved from https://www.shrm.org/resourcesandtools/hr-topics/talent-acquisition/pages/dont-underestimate-the-importance-of-effective-onboarding.aspx.

SECTION 3: Thrive

Chapter 2: Networking Internally and Externally

Littel, B. (2003). *The Heart and Art of NetWeaving*. NetWeaving International Press.

Chapter 8: Finding New Opportunities to Deliver Value

Boyd, John R. (3 September 1976). *Destruction and Creation (PDF)*. U.S. Army Command and General Staff College.

Chapter 9: Giving the Gift of Feedback

Dweck, C. (2017). *Mindset: Changing the way you think to fulfill your potential.* Penguin Random House.

ABOUT THE AUTHORS

Gerald Hutchinson

My path to leadership coaching and consulting came from my adventures in the wilderness. For a few years, I was a wilderness guide taking young adults on backpacking treks in the Appalachian Mountains of North Carolina, and canoeing expeditions in the Florida Everglades. In these intensive ever-changing "leadership laboratories," I got to experiment with leadership styles and tactics, and lead dozens of small teams of 10-14 members for intensive 24/7 experiences of 9- to 90-days.

When I wanted to earn a much-wanted promotion from a Field Instructor to a Course Director, my own manager coached me to better performance. I had to learn to listen more and talk less; to listen for the "vibe" of my team members; and to be more strategic about how I positioned and interacted with students. My success in this role eventually led me to a position as the Director of the Outdoor Leadership Program at Davidson College, teaching student leaders in team leadership using the challenge of overcoming outdoor adventures as the shared common goal.

Realizing that there could be more opportunity for developing better workplaces through leadership by working in the private sector, I enrolled in a Ph.D. program in Counseling Psychology at UNC Greensboro, selecting this program primarily because the Center for Creative Leadership's (CCL) headquarters is in Greensboro. I thought I would be well positioned to get an internship and eventual employment there. But the fates had something else in store: I quickly met a consultant who worked for a competitor of CCL while doing a transformative program in Emotional Intelligence for Executives. After meeting with the founder and the man who became a mentor, Dr. Jim Farr, I was hired to lead intensive emotional intelligence workshops monthly until I could finish my PhD and work as a consultant with Farr Associates. (Twist my arm!)

This behavioral science consulting firm was acquired by BB&T and the mission changed, so another consultant and I left and formed our own firm doing similar but different types of work, with greater emphasis on executive management team development, and coaching high-potential middle managers. Our client-facing consulting was magical, and like many partnerships it was also filled with tension about running the business, and it was clear it would not last. My partner bought me out, and in 2003 I became a sole owner of my own consulting firm.

In 2018 after years working for myself traveling all over the United States serving large corporations, I decided to take my experiences and help smaller, local businesses. I joined with the #1 Business Coaching firm in the world, ActionCOACH®. I love serving smaller clients that do not always have the resources of large corporations for their leadership and organizational development needs.

Throughout my coaching career, I've worked with Fortune 500 Executives, Directors, and thousands of middle managers from companies large and small. I've administered thousands of psychological profiles, and coached people on developing themselves and their leadership. Working with the Macy's Strategic Leaders program is where I met Josh Saterman, an exceptionally gifted human possessing both superb human relations skills and business acumen.

My work is incredibly enriching because when a leader gets better, they have a positive effect on all those around them. This perfectly emphasizes my mission to coach people to BE all that they can be, be smart, and leverage their capabilities to make the world a better place.

Nettie Nitzberg

I grew up in a family of retailers. Retail is in my blood. I spent my childhood, teen, and college years working in the family business. Going on buying trips, merchandising the windows and displays, and of course selling. However, I never had any ambition to continue in the retail industry or so I thought.

Out of college I had no idea what I wanted to do. So, I did what I knew best and began my career in a buying program for a major retailer. I was an assistant buyer, department manager, and then head of display for one of the stores. I was not challenged or energized – and I realized I had to make a change... but what.

My mom was working on her master's degree and was introduced to an organization called American Society of Training and Development (ASTD). I was working as a recruiter in the retail industry, at the time – loving the work I did with candidates to build their resumes and prepare for interviews but not the selling part. Understanding what I enjoyed doing she suggested I attend an ASTD meeting with her. The people I met at the event were doing some cool things - training managers, facilitating workshops, and building teams. The speaker Leonard Nadler, head of the Human Resources Master's Program at George Washington University, spoke about the program, the courses, and professions of the students. I was hooked. Afterwards I spoke with Dr. Nadler about the program, applied, and was accepted two months later. This meeting set the path for my career and passion in developing talent and building organizational culture.

After grad school I worked for Accenture (Andersen Consulting at the time) in their change management group. I loved the training I received through them. The friends I worked with were awesome. I loved being a consultant but did not like building technical training programs. I was meant to be an instructional designer focused on designing and developing professional development initiatives. After two years of learning so many life- and professional skills at Accenture, I changed jobs and used my skills to run the training department at a start-up telecom. I came alive in this role and found my career life path.

Life always has its twists and turns. We moved out of Washington DC and settled in Buffalo, NY (near my hometown of Niagara Falls, NY), and I could not find a full-time job. At this point I had two young children and again returned to something I knew, consulting. In the mid 90's I hung my shingle and started my consulting practice. Little did I know I would build my business in two more cities and run this business for over 25 years.

I love the learning and development field. It allows me to use my talents and strengths in so many ways. No day is the same. No client is the same. No project is the same. I get to be creative and innovate. I can think strategically and roll-up my sleeves. I get to work with all different types of people in a variety of industries. I can stretch myself and learn something new every day. I can teach others, learn from others, collaborate, and build things from the ground up. I have traveled globally and worked with clients around the world. I have learned so much!

When I think back to the beginning of working in the "family" business, little did I know I would run my own business, work with my mom, my brother, my husband, and my daughter. I had no idea I would meet some of the most important people in my life because of my work. Many of my best and dearest friends were/are clients, are collaborators, and thought partners. This is how I met Josh - this is how I met Gerald, and this is how I became an author. I always said, I never wanted to write a book, and again life has its twists and turns. Now I am an author.

Josh Saterman

Over the last few years, I have had the time to pause and reflect. I left my big corporate job, started my journey as an entrepreneur, consultant, coach, and let's set the tone now; I have had to learn (and I'm still learning) how to get comfortable being uncomfortable. Someone once told me, if you aren't a little nauseous, you aren't growing. Of course, my response was, "What happens when I'm really, really nauseous?" But that's a different story ...

How did I get here? Who inspired me? Sometimes it feels like I blinked and BOOM!, I've been transported to the future. What did I learn along the way? Who taught me? Why did it matter?

Along the way, people impacted me, and that imprint continues to be part of my story and learning along the way. This book honors two of my mentors and shares their impact on my career, my perspective on life, and how I plan to pay it forward. Oprah Winfrey said, "A mentor is someone who allows you to see the hope inside yourself."

The first mentor I had was Becky Dannenfelser. While Becky left us too soon, her legacy, wisdom, and spirit have stayed with me. I think of Becky almost every day. She was the first person I knew to leave a big corporate job and become a coach. She dreamed big, pushed hard, and never allowed anything to stand in her way.

Becky would take long walks with me. She would listen to me, support my ideas, and coach me along the way. She never made me feel badly, even when she disagreed and pushed back, rather, she navigated my journey with patience, understanding, compassion, and force. I hope that every day I serve as a coach, I make her a little prouder of my accomplishments and my drive to put people first.

One day I was sitting in another mentor's office and sharing with her a few of my obstacles and concerns regarding a group project. She listened, observed, took notes, and didn't speak until she finally said, "Go back to the group and do two things for me. One, only ask questions that start with 'What' and 'How', and don't tell them any answers. And two, listen with your eyes."

Sometimes the power of coaching is not when the coach or mentor speaks, and instead what the coaching client or mentee hears, sees, and feels from a topic or a conversation. My boss-coach-mentor, Molly Langenstein, reminded me several times on my journey to "listen with my eyes." Her reminder was that people have their perspectives, their priorities, and their perceptions. By watching how they move, hear, sit, have eye contact, as well as the inflection in their voice, you can start to really understand people and their motivating factors more clearly. When you actually hear a person's full message, you can truly become an active listener. When you understand a person or people better, you can start to build unified messaging, find common goals, and establish trust.

The power of a brilliant leader is in their ability to understand what motivates a teammate. A question you can ask yourself when presented with a challenge, "How are my teammates looking at a challenge through their eyes?". How do you help them solve that challenge, or at the least, bridge the gap between you and them? You, as a leader, own the power of translating understanding!

The art of listening is a muscle. Molly pushed me to build that muscle by focusing on how I listen and really hear. She would ask me tough questions. Sometimes she dumbfounded me with her perspective and wisdom. She had the patience for my inquisitive thoughts and always pushed me to dream bigger. Molly would say, "It's tough to dream down." One real power to brilliant coaching is the ability to lift people up.

We grow and we push ourselves to dream up. We can be strong and confident. We don't have all the answers, and that's ok. Great leaders know how to build dynamic teams. Dynamic teams know how to work together and leverage their combined strengths to solve problems. As was said previously, over 50% of people leave their jobs because of their manager. We're all on our journey, and we are leaving you with a few words of wisdom.

Words of wisdom learned

- **You are more than one moment**. Don't let the job, company, task, moment or any other specific time period or moment define you.
- **Stop and listen**. Find a mentor. A guiding light. Someone who believes in you. Sometimes the most powerful words you can say to a person are: "I believe in you."
- **Let people in**. Get vulnerable. Say what's on your mind. Don't apologize for being open and always lead with humility. You're a real person. Your thoughts should be shared.
- **If your boss doesn't listen to you, find someone that will**. Real leaders always put their team first. Leaders always make time to ensure their team finds the way.
- **Love people**. Learn about people. Respect their motivators. Share what lights your way and listen to what lights their way. Lift people up by asking them great questions.
- **Honor your mentors**. People aren't perfect; they make mistakes. Perfection is not the goal; rather, the goal is aspiring to become a lifetime learner by getting better every day. Listen to those who provide guidance. After all, it's guidance not gospel.
- **Have an open mind**. You never know when you might learn something new.
- **Breathe**. Just Breathe.

From that coaching moment with Molly (and many others), I was promoted four times over the next six years. She believed in me, and that belief inspired me to do better, be better, and rise to the occasion.

I still have the desire to make both Becky and Molly proud. I want them to know they made a difference not just in my career, and more importantly, in my life.

Both Becky and Molly are now part of my forever journey and the way I coach and look to be coached. They unlocked parts within me that I might not have seen on my own. This is one of the many powers in becoming a brilliant coach. As I continue my coaching, consulting, and leadership journey, I hope to provide this same guidance, respect and energy for others.

What type of legacy do you want to leave? Who will you mentor, sponsor, coach, invest in starting today? And of course, the most important lesson is that successful **people never reach their goals alone.**

How Josh met Gerald and Nettie...

If memory serves me, I met Gerald unexpectedly. I had just been accepted into my company's senior level of leadership training program. I was moving up in the corporate world and the company picked two people out of my entire division of more than 1200 people to participate in this nine-month leadership program. Part of this program was working with an executive coach. The purpose of this executive coach was to support your development through goal setting and establishing accountability partners. This sentiment partially comes from the book and adage, "What got you here, won't get you there" by Marshall Goldsmith. Like many of you, you will have the opportunity to be placed with an executive coach. Remember, coaching can change your life.

Over the course of the next several years, Gerald and I would coach, partner, collaborate, and connect. Now, we are friends and colleagues. In this book, we discuss leadership and the learning journey that you will create for yourself as part of your corporate or corporate adjacent journey. We are excited to share our learnings and our experiences to support you in your leadership development.

For me, Gerald was a crucial part of my journey and our journeys continue. Your journey is happening right now. This book is a continuation of that journey and why not share that journey with others. As we've mentioned and will continue mentioning, "we learn about ourselves by experiencing other people's stories".

And so here we are. In 2019, Gerald and I decided to co-write a book. We combined our experiences to share with you our thoughts, tools, and experiences to support emerging leaders.

And yet, there was a piece missing... Nettie Nitzberg.

I met Nettie 18 years ago when my husband and Nettie started working together. One night we had dinner together. We quickly realized that we had so much in common from our art to our taste in colors. Since then, we've grown together, traveled the world, and have been there for each other during some of life's most challenging moments. Oh, and we both enjoy wine! Nettie being a high WOO (strengths talent theme), and me being a high Maximizer (another strengths talent theme) started to work on consulting projects together, thinking about ways to take our experiences, and share them with clients.

Boom. In 2020, Nettie joined Saterman Connect as a managing partner and the trifecta of Josh, Gerald, and Nettie as co-authors for this book was born. While Gerald owns his own firm, ANOVA Performance Solutions LLC, this trifecta works together through the various projects and clients they serve.

ARRIVE. DRIVE. THRIVE.™ was a natural evolution among us to support aspiring, emerging, and existing leaders with their leadership journey.

ABOUT OUR BUSINESSES

Saterman Connect

Our mission is to unlock your organization's full potential, beginning with your people. Whether we are focused on developing and growing leaders, helping you define your business or learning strategy, or tackling bold conversations around diversity, equity, inclusion, and belonging, it all starts with you listening to and empowering your people.

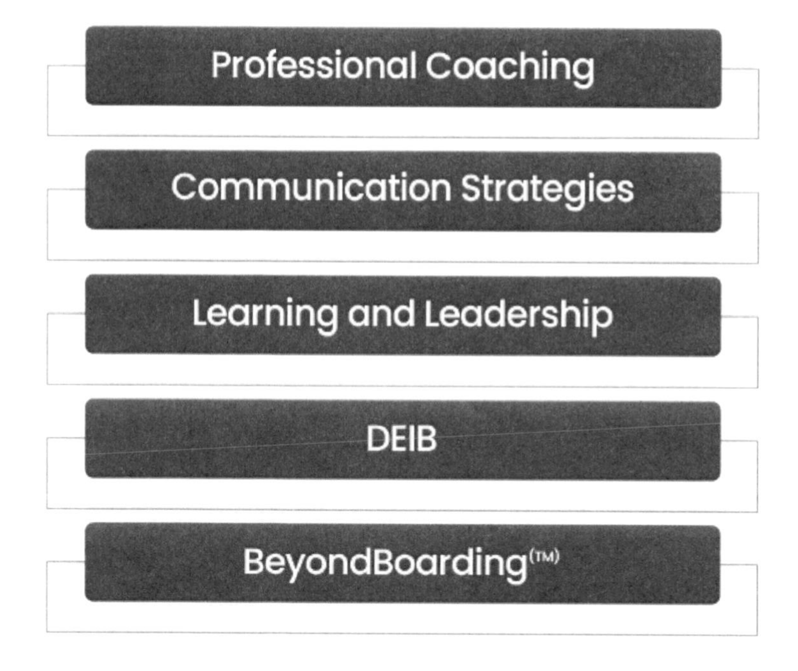

Contact us at **SatermanConnect.com**

Gerald Hutchinson, The Business Excellerator™ Certified ActionCOACH®

For over 25 years, our commitment has been to help business owners and managers work smarter, build systems to help them perform better with less effort and waste, and build high-performing teams.

We provide coaching for business owners and managers who want to actively get better at:

- Marketing and Sales
- Financial Discipline
- Streamlining Operations
- Customer Service
- Leading Teams Effectively
- Time and Priority Management
- Mindsets for Sustaining Success
- Innovation and Problem-Solving

Contact Gerald at *geraldhutchinson@actioncoach.com*

Bring your leadership journey into your organization through the Arrive. Drive. Thrive.™ Leadership Academy.